The Ellison's

SEEDS
FROM · THE
SOWER

SEEDS
FROM · THE
SOWER

The Michael and Audrey Guido Story

How God is blessing a couple who dare to take Him at His Word

MICHAEL AND AUDREY GUIDO

MICHAEL GUIDO
with SARAH COLEMAN

THOMAS NELSON PUBLISHERS

NASHVILLE

Unless otherwise noted, Scripture quotations are from THE NEW KING JAMES VERSION. Copyright © 1979, 1980, 1982, Thomas Nelson, Inc., Publishers.

Scripture quotations noted NIV are from The Holy Bible: NEW INTERNATIONAL VERSION. Copyright © 1978 by the New York International Bible Society. Used by permission of Zondervan Publishers.

Scripture quotations noted NASB are from THE NEW AMERICAN STANDARD BIBLE, Copyright © 1960, 1962, 1963, 1968, 1971, 1972, 1973, 1975, 1977 by The Lockman Foundation and are used by permission.

Scripture quotations noted TLB are from *The Living Bible* (Wheaton, Illinois: Tyndale House Publishers, 1971) and are used by permission.

Scripture quotations noted KJV are from The Holy Bible: King James Version. Copyright © 1983, Thomas Nelson, Inc., Publishers.

Library of Congress Cataloging-in-Publication Data

Guido, Michael.
  Seeds from the sower : the Michael and Audrey Guido story /
Michael and Audrey Guido ; with Sarah Coleman.
    p.   cm.
  ISBN 0-8407-3178-7
  1. Guido, Michael.   2. Guido, Audrey.   3. Evangelists—United
States—Biography.   4. Guido Evangelistic Association.   5. Mass
media in missionary work.   I. Guido, Audrey.   II. Coleman, Sarah
Jepson.   III. Title.
BV3780.G85A3   1990
269'.2'0922—dc20
[B]

90-40077
CIP

This book is lovingly dedicated to Audrey, my leading lady for forty-seven years. She has made my life pleasurable and my labor profitable. She daily brings me new hope and help that no one else on earth can give. She is an integral part of this work, managing my life and our ministry. She has mastered the production side of radio, television, and print. She sows prayerfully, quietly, and professionally, knowing her work for the Lord will endure.

CONTENTS

PART FOUR

ACKNOWLEDGMENTS

MY THANKFUL ACKNOWLEDGMENT is made to Thomas Nelson, Inc., for working with me in the publication of this book. I am grateful to them for introducing to me the heart-moving writing of my skillful scribe, Sarah Coleman.

A wonderful circle of caring comprised those who contributed to research. My own staff were attentive and encouraging. Many of our board members audited the project with interest.

Residents and merchants in Metter, Georgia, shared their memories. Station managers and listeners poured out their stories of what The Sower outreach for the Savior has meant in their lives. Research became a source of joy to Audrey and me.

I am a product of Moody Bible Institute and its staff of dedicated people. Great men, like Dr. Will Houghton and William W. Shannon, invested themselves in me. Much of my continuing education comes from the books and teaching of people who stayed close to God and were taught by the Spirit. My writings reflect their written and spoken words. It would be impossible to footnote their indelible impression on me and our ministry.

Standards of excellence came from my mother and Audrey's mother, and both of our fathers exemplified stability in the midst of adversity. Family is precious to us, and we honor the memory of those with the Lord and thank Him for the ones remaining. They become touchstones of the past and a blessing to the present.

Thank you, and may God lavishly bless you all!

FOREWORD

WHEN I WAS asked to write the foreword for *Seeds from the Sower*, I thought to myself, *Just another book for the country-club evangelical set*.

How wrong I was!

When I started to read the manuscript, I did not stop until I finished every word. I could not put it down. It was like reading the "Acts of the Apostles"—one miracle after another; one answer to prayer after another. I was fascinated by the various situations in which God answered prayer, supplied needs, and provided incredibly at the very point of despair.

I have been aware of the unique ministry of Michael and Audrey Guido of the Guido Evangelistic Association, Metter, Georgia, since 1959. At that time I first heard the radio program "The Sower," as Director of Radio for TransWorld Radio, Chatham, New Jersey, and Monte Carlo, Monaco, and was impressed by the excellence of message and technical quality of the program.

In 1982 I had the privilege of presenting a Citation of Honor to the Guidos at their 25th anniversary of the ministry. What a dramatic increase in depth and scope over that period! When interviewed over radio about a program called "A Seed for the

Garden of Your Heart," I said emphatically that it was "a positive program with broad appeal to every segment of the population," and in technology one of the "finest programs seen on television, produced on location in a garden setting in Metter, Georgia."

No one can read *Seeds from the Sower* without stretching to new heights of spiritual dimension.

The co-author has captured the heartbeat of both Michael and Audrey with honest poignancy and rugged realism. Not a lot of fancy concepts, but a straightforward, up-front description of what actually happened.

From the depths of pain to the heights of success, Michael and Audrey exemplify what God can accomplish through humble people who dedicate themselves to the Lord Jesus Christ, and all this with quiet abandon to the leading of the Holy Spirit.

My spiritual horizons were raised immeasurably by reading this book.

Now it's your turn.

Ben Armstrong
Executive Director, Thirty Years
National Religious Broadcasters

"THE SOWER"

A stained glass window D. L. Moody placed at the Moody Bible Institute in 1889. It was designed from a painting by Jean Francois Millet.

PART ONE

CHAPTER 1

SOWING
IN THE
MORNING

Oh satisfy us in the morning *with thy likeness*
That we may sing for joy and be glad all our days.
Psalm 90:14, NAS

With a thousand-watt smile and all the energy and
exuberance of a nineteen-year-old, Michael Guido sprinted
up the steps of the Moody Bible Institute. It was his first
day. Little did he envision that in years to come he would
be heard by a potential listening audience of more than
100 million American households, plus countless foreign
outlets. Nor was he aware that forty-eight years later he
would become Moody's Alumnus of the Year, an award
earned by Christian service, character, and loyalty to
God's Word.

In the lobby of Crowell Hall, behind the information
desk, he caught a compelling glimpse of a stained glass
window that would forever remain etched in his heart. It
was titled *The Sower*. Located at 153 Institute Place in
Chicago, and placed there by Dwight L. Moody himself,
it had been copied from an oil painting by French artist
Jean Francois Millet. Tradition has it that *The Sower* was a
favorite subject of Mr. Moody's, both orally and in his
writings. Consistently he urged Christian workers to sow
the "precious seeds of faith in Jesus Christ."

Michael Guido would become a dedicated sower of good

seed. Coming to the Institute as a former dance band member and leader, his life of faith parallels that of George Muller and portrays his implicit trust in the Lord.

Before Michael was born, his father emigrated from Naples, Italy, looking for the land of liberty and opportunity, determined to make any sacrifice necessary to become an American. He left home at age fifteen and found a job on an oceangoing ship sailing for the United States. He was urged to go to Lorain, Ohio, where the Baltimore and Ohio Railroad hired men to work on the section gang.

In Lorain he met a fellow Italian, who was the railroad foreman and who gave him his first job. The boss's daughter would become his bride and Michael, their firstborn son.

Michael was named for two saints of the Roman Catholic Church—St. Michael and St. Anthony. Today he is quick to quip that his name never made him saintly. But his parents were intent on guiding him in the right direction, so nuns and priests visited the home frequently.

The parents were poor, and many Christmases, as the family grew, the only gifts were cookies and cakes that Mother made. Father still worked for the Baltimore and Ohio, which was known as the B&O. To the kids that meant "Beans and Onions" because they could not afford other foods. The clothes and bread were homemade, and with no money for bus fare, the children walked the five miles to school. Since they saw this as an opportunity to strengthen their young bodies, not a disgrace or a disappointment, there was no complaining.

Michael's mother was very devoted to her church—until the day she was invited to attend a revival meeting five miles from home. She was aware that her husband would never allow her to darken the door of a protestant church, yet an inward tug drew her to this Methodist meeting on an evening when Michael's father was working overtime. When she came home the family noticed a discernible change.

The next day she gathered her children around her and

told them she had received the Lord Jesus as her Savior and had been born again. They had never heard such words from their mother. They could not understand, but they all saw an unexplainable beauty emerge in her life.

Michael describes the changes that took place as the result of a faithful witness who *sowed the seeds of God's love* in his mother by inviting her to hear the Word.

WHEN PA CAME home from work the next evening, Ma told him of her conversion. He became very angry and threatened to divorce her if she ever went to a protestant church again. Her parents, sisters, and brothers became concerned too. Members of our Catholic church did their best to persuade Ma to come back, but to no avail.

Ma went to her room every Friday, leaving word that we were not to disturb her except for an emergency, and she fasted and prayed all day until Pa came home from work. She didn't neglect us on that day, for she always had homemade bread and cookies for us, and something in the refrigerator.

Because of the winsome change in my mother, I wanted to go to a church. After attending Mass, I came home and said, "Pa, I went to our church. You wouldn't mind if I go to that little Baptist church around the corner from our house, would you?" He gave permission for "just this once."

Imagine my first experience in a protestant church. I looked for the holy water, but couldn't find it. I came to the pew and was about to kneel to pray when the kids around me started to giggle. I went into the pew and looked for the kneeling bench, which, of course, was not there. And the church was so noisy! I was terribly disappointed and disgusted at the irreverence.

After the opening exercises, I was led into the Sunday school room. The teacher, a schoolteacher, welcomed me warmly; and she taught the Bible lesson so beautifully that she made me hungry to come back. I was deeply impressed with that part of the service and was thrilled with the music and message of the morning worship. How I wished I could go every Sunday, but I knew I could not.

However, Ma was very faithful in living Christ before us. Lovingly, she made us hungry to become Christians. When Pa was on strike, Ma got a job cleaning that little Baptist church, and my sisters and I enjoyed helping her every Saturday. That gave us a good excuse to go there, and Pa was in favor, for we needed the money desperately.

As I was walking home from a theater one Sunday afternoon when I was eighteen years old, I was attracted by the singing coming from a meeting in an abandoned store on Broadway where two Baptist pastors were conducting a revival. The music arrested me, and in I went.

The ushers recognized me, and wanted to get me as close to the front as possible. But I said, "No, give me a seat by the door. As soon as the singing is over, I'm leaving."

Sitting by the door, I enjoyed that heartwarming singing. And when it was over, I couldn't leave. I felt frozen in that seat.

The preacher preached about the love of our Lord. He melted my heart. It was not hell and its horribleness that led me to the Lord. It was God's love. When the invitation was given, and the congregation was singing "Just as I Am," I wanted to go forward, but I was afraid. I knew it would break my father's heart, and I loved him too much for that. I knew I'd have to give up my vocation, and I enjoyed it too much for that. But the Spirit of God wooed and won my heart. I went forward. I fell to my knees and I cried: "Lord Jesus, Thou didst die for me; I'll live for Thee. Thy hands and Thy feet were nailed to the cross for me; I give Thee my hands and my feet. Thy body was broken for me; I give Thee my body. Live Thy life all over again in me. I'll live for Thee. Yes, Lord, if need be, I'll die for Thee. Just save me and have Thy way with me."

That was the greatest night of my life!

Folks have asked, "Did you get a feeling when you were saved?" Did I! Someone hurried to our home and told my father about my conversion. He was waiting for me and gave me a very warm reception. And he was patriotic—he used stripes and I saw stars! But it was worth it all, and I was glad I could suffer a little for my Lord.

My former grade school teacher, the Sunday school teacher who had blessed my heart on my first visit to the protestant church, heard about my conversion and brought me a beautiful, leather-bound Bible. Our priest heard about it, and he didn't want me to read it. (I'm glad the Catholic church has changed.) He told my father to search for it and burn it. He urged him to do his best to keep us from reading it, even if he had to beat us.

By this time, we had led my three sisters to the Lord, and Mother wanted us to have a family altar. We couldn't have it during the day because we were in school. Pa came home from work about the same time we came home from school, so we couldn't have it then. Pa never went out with the fellows in the evening. He spent every night at home, so we couldn't read the Bible then. Here is how we had our family altar. After we had all gone to bed, Pa was the first to fall asleep, and he always slept soundly. When she heard him snore, Ma came to my room. We called the girls in, locked the door, turned on a dim light, took the Bible from its hiding place, and gathered around Ma's knees as she read to us. That is where I got my love for the Bible.

Ma, the three girls, and I felt that we should be baptized. Pa was determined to keep us from doing it. He felt that baptism would take us from the Catholic church permanently, so he did everything he could to stop us.

On the Sunday we wanted to be baptized, Pa drank heavily. (In our large wine cellar with three-foot-thick stone walls, we had our own wine press, and every year made barrels of wine from the tons of grapes trucked in.) Pa threatened us and then thrashed us. Then he locked the doors, put the keys in his pocket, and fell asleep. While he was sleeping soundly that evening, I slipped the keys out of his pocket. We ran out of the house and started to walk to the church.

Ma, who had heart trouble, was quite ill. I was terribly concerned for her. We came to 23rd Street and Broadway and paused at the corner. The rays of the streetlight fell on my mother's face, and I saw that she was in deep pain. Standing in front of her, I said, "Ma, with your heart trouble, the doctor said the least excitement could bring on an attack. When we get home, Pa will beat us unmercifully. Do we have to go through with it? Can't we be secret Christians? Can't we be silent believers? Do we have to go all the way?"

Stretching her arms around us, she said, "Children, we are going all the way or not at all."

We went all the way. And I'm grateful. For we have had the

joy of leading all of our loved ones to the Lord. That night I realized the importance of going "all the way or not at all." What a lesson I learned! It has stirred me to go "all the way" ever since that decision.

While I could play several instruments, I could not sing. One day I read in the Bible how the Lord made a donkey talk. Immediately I prayed, "Lord, if You can make a donkey talk, You can give me a voice and make me a singer. So, thanks, Lord!"

A few days later, the gentleman who played the piano during the revival in which I was saved, came to me and said, "Michael, I believe the Lord wants you to be a singer and a song leader. Let's try out your voice."

"Great!" I said.

He played the introduction to a gospel song and said, "Sing it!" I was thrilled, so thrilled that I cried. The Lord had heard my prayer. Mr. Brown then said, "I'm booking you to sing next Friday night. We'll pick you up at 6:30."

On that Friday we had dinner as usual. As soon as we had finished eating, while my father was enjoying his wine, I said, "Pa, they want me to sing in a little Methodist church out in the country. You don't care if I go, do you?"

Jumping to his feet, turning red with rage, he shouted, "Tonight you must decide between your father and your new faith. Which will it be?"

Turning to my mother I asked, "Ma, shall I go?"

"Son," she replied, "put Jesus before your mother and father; put Him first in your life." With that, my father struck her, and she fell to the floor, bleeding.

As I stepped forward to help her, he prevented me. "Tonight," he said, "you must make that decision. If you go and sing, you can't ever come back home. What is your decision?"

Slipping into a coat, I started to sing, "Jesus, I my cross have taken." My father cursed me, slammed the door, and shouted, "You can't come home tonight!" As I walked out the door with the pain of a desperate decision, that song's words brought healing to a very young man's brokenness:

> Jesus, I my cross have taken,
> All to leave and follow Thee;

Destitute, despised, forsaken.
Thou, from hence, my all shalt be.
Perish every fond ambition,
All I've sought, and hoped, and known;
Yet how rich is my condition,
God and heaven are still my own!

That night I sang my first solo. Coming home in the car with the gospel team, I started to cry.

"What's wrong?" asked a friend.

"I have no home to go to," I sobbed.

He started to sing, and the others joined in, "Be not dismayed what e'er betide, God will take care of you." Oh, that was the sweetest thing I had ever heard. "Sing it again, fellows," I begged. And they did. How it comforted me. At our house they let me out. My father was seated in a chair, drinking his wine, and smoking his pipe. Anger was written all over his face.

We lived at 32nd Street on Broadway, and that night as I walked down to Lake Erie and back, the Lord drew near and walked with me and talked with me, calling me to go all the way. Confrontations with Pa were not infrequent. I crept back in the house after he was asleep, unsure of him but assured of the presence of Jesus right there beside me.

Soon friends were urging me to train for Christian work, and some took me to various Christian colleges. Not one really won my heart. Then someone mentioned Moody Bible Institute. That rang a bell. The more I thought about Moody, the more I felt the Lord wanted me there.

Immediately after dinner on the day I made that decision, I announced to the family, "Lord willing, I'm going to the Moody Bible Institute in Chicago to train for Christian work."

"Over my dead body!" shouted my father. And he laid a whipping on me, even though I was nineteen. But that did not bother me. Rather it blessed me—it drove me to my knees in prayer, and it drew me closer to Christ.

One afternoon about a week later, to my utter amazement, my father said, "Are you still determined to go to Moody?"

"Yes, sir," I answered.

"Suppose I get you a pass on the Nickel Plate Railroad?"

What an answer to prayer. I didn't have any money for the trip. Oh, you can't beat Jesus, can you?

A few weeks later I went to Moody, high in faith but low on funds. I had twenty-five dollars and a two-piece suit—a piece of one and a piece of another. They say there's a shiny side to everything. There surely was to that suit. However, I was confident and cheerful, looking not at my meager resources but at the richness of my new faith.

Arriving in Chicago about seven one morning, I got off the train and asked how to get to the Moody Bible Institute. A redcap told me, and I began to walk.

Sometime later, I stood in the lobby, absorbing the impact of *The Sower,* that magnificent stained glass window, and recalling the incidents that brought me here. I was directed to see the superintendent of men Mr. Davis, whom I found to be a wonderfully kind Christian gentleman.

I said, "Please, sir, I'd like to become a student."

"Fine," he said. "Have you been accepted as a student?"

"No, sir," I confessed.

"Do you have $150?"

"No, sir," I answered. "I have ten dollars."

"Son," he advised, "why don't you get a job for your room and board and come to evening school?"

I promised to try. It was in 1933 when everybody and his brother wanted a job and could not get one. A dentist offered me bed and breakfast in return for washing his windows in a big building. Looking down from the tall building as I washed the windows made me awfully dizzy. This high hope for a job was too high—I couldn't do it.

I went back to see Mr. Davis and asked for his help. The gracious man said, "Here's a recommendation to a Thompson Restaurant. Give it to the manager, and I'm sure you will get a job."

Sure enough, it worked just like he said.

I will never forget my first day of work, bussing dishes. My tray was loaded with china and silverware when the manager came up to me and said, "I like the way you smile broadly at my customers and treat them courteously. Have you ever bussed dishes before?"

"No, sir," I said. And I proved it. I dropped the tray, "busting" all the dishes.

"Son," he advised, "eat your free meal, and don't come back!"

I ate and hurried back to see the superintendent of men. "Mr. Davis," I said, "it worked. Your recommendation got me a job."

"Good!" he exclaimed.

"But I was fired," I sadly admitted.

"Michael," he asked, "do you have any friends at home who will help you?"

"I'm not sure," I answered.

"Have you ever trusted the Lord for your daily needs before?" he wondered.

"No," I replied, "but I'm anxious to trust Him now."

I was given a key to a single room, and I got down on my knees and prayed, "Lord Jesus, I've tried to find work, but I have failed. But I will spend all the time in prayer that I would have spent at work if You will meet my needs." I did, and He proved faithful!

One day I was shining my shoes with the polish Moody provided the students. I looked at my right shoe and I said, "Lord, look at that. Tonight I am going to sing "I'm a Child of the King," and my toe sticks out of my shoe. The congregation will think that I am a liar or You are a sorry King. Please give me a pair of shoes." Just as soon as I walked out of the room, an evening student named Hans Stalder met me and asked if I needed a pair of shoes. Did I! I held up my right foot and wiggled the toe. Hans escorted me to a store and bought me a pair of shoes.

Trying to make a decision, I prayed silently, "Lord Jesus, reveal to me which color I should buy." The clerk brought out a gray pair, a color I had never worn before, and the Lord seemed to say these were right. The clerk wrapped the old shoes, and I wore the new ones.

While I waited at a corner for the light to change, a man said, "I like your gray shoes."

"Thank you," I replied. "I like yours too. Are you walking with the Lord?"

"No," he admitted, "but I'd like to." There on the street corner I led him to the Lord Jesus. My heart was full of joy—a seed had brought forth fruit.

Another student asked to borrow the only razor blade I had. "You may borrow it," I said, "but please bring it back. I don't have another."

When he told me he had dropped it on the way to return it, I stood in front of the mirror and said, "Lord, look at my face. I need a shave, and I don't have any blades. Please send me one." The next day I received two razor blades in the mail. They came from Mr. Brown, the musician who led me into singing. He kept on sending razor blades until I graduated from Moody. He was such a sharp friend.

Meanwhile my suit was becoming—well—worn out. I needed one desperately. So I prayed, "Lord Jesus, I need a suit. I'm ashamed of this one. If You want me to keep on wearing it a little longer, I will. But won't You please give me one soon?"

A day or two later a friend asked me to take a walk with him. I agreed and said, "We'll pass out tracts going to town."

We came to a clothing store, and he said, "I have a salesman I'd like for you to meet." He introduced me to his friend, and the two of them talked a little while. Then he asked, "If you were buying a suit, what would you get?"

"A double-breasted oxford gray," I replied. Presently, the salesman brought out just what I had described and instructed me to try it on for size. I could hardly get into it because of my tears.

Many students asked me to pray for their requests, both spoken and unspoken. One day a young lady asked me to pray for an unspoken request, and I assured her that I would.

"It's very urgent," she insisted.

"I will pray often and fervently," I responded.

About a month later, D. L. Foster, a teacher whom I greatly admired, called me into his office and asked about this young lady's unspoken request. "Are you praying for it?" he questioned.

"With all my heart," I assured him.

"Would you like to know what it is?" he asked. He had such a twinkle in his eyes that I blurted out, yes, I would like to know. He said, "This girl is praying that you fall in love with her and marry her."

"Lord," I hastened to pray, "cancel the order!" Sometimes I am grateful for unanswered prayer. For the Lord had a choice lady—a Georgia peach—in mind for me. She would one day make my life full and complete.

To remind me to make everything a matter of prayer, I made a sign that I hung around the handle on the inside of my door at Moody's. It read: *Have You Prayed about It?* Every time I turned the knob to open the door, I saw the sign. If I had not prayed about what I was going to do, the sign reminded me to drop to my knees and pray. That helped train me to never do anything without prayer.

Now, almost six decades later, I never leave our home, my study, or our studio, or get into a car, without praying about what I'm going to do. When the phone rings and my secretary tells me who wants to speak to me, before I pick up the receiver, I ask the Lord for His wisdom for everything we will talk about, and I ask Him to make me a blessing to the caller.

On hearing an ambulance siren, I pray for the driver, the medic, the nurse, and the patient. On hearing the siren of a fire truck, I lift a prayer to the Lord for the firefighters, for their safety, for success in battling the blaze, and for the others involved. On hearing the siren of a police car, I call on the Lord to protect the peace officer, to grant wisdom in dealing with the situation, and to begin working for the salvation of the one in trouble.

On reading the morning papers, I look over the obituary column and lift a prayer for the bereaved families. When I see the name of our president, governor, mayor, senator, a member of Congress, a preacher, or a broken soul, I look to the Lord to minister to the need of that public servant. Every time I think of a board member and his family or any friend, I quickly call upon the Lord to help. There is nothing like these quick-calls or heavenly telegrams that are lifted when the struggle is the fiercest and the need the greatest.

How real life's experiences are to me—even today.

Few students had money at Bible school. But Michael was learning the uncommon language of God's heart. The prayer of Jehoshaphat was his also: "Neither know we

what to do, but our eyes are upon thee (2 Chron. 20:12,
KJV).

He recognized his chief help was prayer. It brought him
the Lord's fatherly blessing and provision.

Teachers at Moody had profound impact on his life. He
still remembers the influences of Dr. Gray, Dr. Fitzwater,
Dr. Weust, and Mr. Bittikofer.

He started his ministry career because of Dr. Will
Houghton, then president of Moody. It happened that
Michael led the singing for him in Florida. One day
before a youth meeting Dr. Houghton said, "Michael, *you*
are going to preach, and I'll lead the singing."

Michael protested, "Oh, no, sir. You are wrong."

"You do not tell your boss he is wrong."

"I don't, sir," Michael meekly responded.

"Go to your room, get down on your knees," Dr.
Houghton continued, "and ask the Lord to give you a
message." The song leader changed roles with a great man
who had become his mentor. After the service, the wise
senior man of God said, "You will no longer be leading
the singing. I know the Lord wants you to preach."

And he did!

The story of Michael Guido unfolds in the pages to
follow. He is indeed a twentieth-century sower, traveling
toward the twenty-first!

His life is a narrative of more than three-quarters of a
century of faith, hope, perseverance, and love.
Meticulously, with his lady, he spreads spiritual seeds,
planted by combining old-world preciseness with the latest
in contemporary technology.

The Sower epitomizes courage and character displayed
in every aspect of life and ministry. He and his wife are a
touching human celebration of faith at work and love in
action. By example they both admonish us to go and do
likewise. They remind us of St. Francis proclaiming to his
students to "Preach the gospel in everything you do. Only
use words when you must."

Sowing in the morning? Yes, and twenty-four hours a

day, every day. He never loses sight of the future for those who have not settled their eternal destinies. Nor does he forget that he is a product of God's love and of a mother who learned the fine art of sowing seeds of kindness.

CHAPTER 2

SOWING
SEEDS OF
KINDNESS

But the fruit of the Spirit is . . . kindness. . . . How precious is Your lovingkindness, O God. . . . Your lovingkindness is better than life. . . . Put on kindness.

Galatians 5:22, Phillips;
Psalms 36:7, 63:3; Colossians 3:12

Washington Irving said, "A kind heart is a fountain of gladness, making everything in its vicinity freshen into smiles." Michael's mother, living in her husband's wrath because of her conversion, and being disowned and discouraged in her faith by her loved ones, continued to express kindness. Her contagious love for Jesus brightened every room.

She and the children were deeply burdened for Father to become a Christian. They knew God would keep His promises, and someday the whole family would be part of God's forever family.

One day Michael suggested, "In music we have grace notes. They are not essential to a score of music, but they are added as something extra to make the score a bit more beautiful. Let's use grace notes to lead Pa to Jesus."

The response was unanimous! When Father came home from work the kids ran to meet him at the corner. One took his lunch bucket, another his coat. At home one would take off his work shoes and help him into his slippers. In summer they made cold lemonade for him and in the winter brought him hot coffee. How? Very lovingly! Mother Guido would cook the food he especially liked with his favorite cakes and pies, even though money continued to be scarce. The family shared the kind of news he was interested in. This touched his heart deeply, and yet the spiritual core of that heart hardened against God.

Some evenings Christian friends came to the home. The family, minus Dad, gathered around the piano and sang and played hymns. Some nights when Father became angry he went down into the basement and threw the main light switch, leaving the group above in darkness. The Christians who had come to visit could not understand his behavior. The little Italian family were shamed, but in the darkness they still wanted the inner lights of their lives to shine. They reminded the Lord that if ever anyone needed a light in a dark place, it was in their pa.

Mrs. Guido bore the brunt of persecution. She was beaten many times for receiving Jesus as her Savior. Her friends said, "Julia, give up your newfound faith. Go back. It is too hard. You cannot stand it. It is killing you. It is going to break your children. Go back."

Smiling kindly, she replied, "I can't." And when her friends persisted, she quietly answered their "why not?" by sharing, "His love won't let me go," and then quoting the lyrics of an old song:

> O Love that wilt not let me go,
> I rest my weary soul in Thee;
> I give Thee back the life I owe,
> That in Thine ocean depths its flow
> May richer, fuller be.

George Matheson had written those words in the mid-nineteenth century when at age twenty, engaged to be married, he learned he was going permanently blind. His fiancée left him. He wrote from a heart of pain, yet confident in his Lord. Julia Guido whispered the words on many occasions:

> O Joy that seekest me through pain,
> I cannot close my heart to Thee;
> I trace the rainbow through the rain,
> And feel the promise is not vain
> That morn shall tearless be.

Michael relates:

HOW SHE ENCOURAGED us! I kept feeling the Lord was calling me into His service, but I didn't feel worthy. I felt the Lord could never use me. One day I read again how He had ridden a donkey into Jerusalem, and I prayed, "Lord, if a donkey could carry You, why can't I? Lord Jesus, please use me."

Later he learned from the writings of George Muller not to let your sense of unworthiness keep you from believing what God has said concerning you. If you are a believer in the Lord Jesus, then this precious privilege of partnership with the Father and the Son is yours.

The grace notes that Michael impressed on his brother and sisters to help win their father came as a result of his music education and his mother's desire that the children become serious musicians. She was kind but firm!

WHEN I WAS about six, my mother wanted me to start taking music lessons. Her sister was a good violinist, so Mother did without food and nice dresses to buy me a violin and give me music lessons with a gifted teacher who charged $1.50 an hour.

I was not too enthusiastic about studying the violin. Drawing the tail of a horse over the gut of a cat did not thrill me as much as being with the boys, and I did not want to practice an hour every day.

One day my mother was terribly exasperated. After begging me, with tears running down her face, to practice, she became a bit angry, and she broke the violin over my head. Boy, was I glad I wasn't taking piano lessons!

When I saw my mother's desire that I play the violin and when I learned of the sacrifice she was making to provide my lessons, my heart was broken. I promised that I would practice, and I did odd jobs to help while mother made more sacrifices—she bought another violin for me.

She did not have to beg me to practice after that experience. All she had to do was hold up that broken violin, and I practiced diligently. And with practice and improvement I began to enjoy playing.

The Lord blessed our home with three girls: Roxanne, whom we called Roxie; Antoinette, whom we called Tonie; and Margaret, whom we called Margie.

Mother kept encouraging their instrumental training, and she made more sacrifices. She bought a piano for Roxie, a cello for Tonie, and a trombone for Margie; and she gave them lessons with choice teachers. I don't know how she did this on the forty cents an hour that my father made.

Each one of us had to practice an hour a day. It must have been hard on my parents, listening daily to four budding musicians.

Being the oldest, I was to teach the others how to do dishes, scrub floors, and clean the house, which Mother kept immaculate. Roxie did not like housework, and to avoid it, she would say she had to practice. We had to do her share of the housework, but we made sure she did practice. And it paid off. She became a great gospel pianist.

My father was not musical, but Mother was determined to play the piano. Roxie taught her, and I can still see her practicing, holding Margie with one hand and playing with the other.

It was fun playing with my sisters. Each of us became a good musician. We enjoyed playing together in our home.

Later on, when I branched out to other instruments, my father made me go to the garage to practice the tuba and trumpet.

My brother, Lawrence—we call him Larry—was born much

later in my parents' lives. About twenty years my junior, he started playing the piano and trombone early. One day Mother heard some strange sounds coming from the bedroom. She ran in and discovered Larry, lying on his back, sliding the trombone with his foot, holding a comic book in his hands and enjoying it. What a time Mother had with us kids! We were rascals.

Wanting to buy a new violin, and knowing my parents could not afford it, I got a job one summer digging ditches—in a cemetery. How I bragged to my friends about having a hundred people under me on my new job.

After I had worked two months, a fellow ditchdigger said, "Michael, you and I weren't built for this backbreaking job. Let's start a dance band."

"You're on," I replied. We got a band together—a good one—and we started playing for church and school dances, and then we went on to dance halls, nightclubs, and vaudeville and burlesque shows. I was about eighteen when I did this.

Pa didn't mind; we needed the money. But it broke Ma's heart. When I came home in the wee hours of the morning, Ma was never in bed. With a shawl around her shoulders, she was on her knees, and I heard her praying for me. Walking up the steps to my bedroom, I could hear "Lord Jesus, You can damn my soul; only save Michael's soul. Lord, You can send me to hell; only save Michael." I would go to my room, not to sleep but to cry over my wickedness.

Ma kept making bread every day. I would slip into the kitchen while she kneaded the dough, and I heard her pray, "Lord Jesus, give my children and my husband a hunger for Thy word. You know how they love my bread; O Jesus, give them a greater hunger for the bread of life."

Ma made our clothes from hand-me-downs, and many times when I walked into the kitchen when she was darning my socks, I heard her pray, "Lord Jesus, lead the feet of my family to Calvary. Save them, and help them to walk in Thy ways."

Many times while she was doing the laundry, I heard her praying as she knelt beside a pile of dirty clothes in the cellar, "Lord Jesus, just as the soap, the water, and the washer will wash these clothes, so by Thy blood, wash away the sins of my family and keep all our lives clean. Lord, I'll gladly go to hell for them; only save them."

No wonder the Lord saved us! How she claimed Acts 16:31: "Believe on the Lord Jesus Christ, and you will be saved, *you and your house*." Often I heard her pray and strongly cry, "I believe Lord Jesus. Now save my house." And He did!

That little orchestra at home led to vast opportunities. Invitations for Michael to play were multiplying. Yet that Sunday afternoon, when he had finished playing at the theater and passed the little church, the Holy Spirit brought genuine conviction. Mother Guido wept when she learned that her son, a new believer, was going to continue to lead the dance band and stay on the theater circuit. Michael sought counsel with a church member. Reassured that it was all right, he went on with his plans to play for a scheduled dance.

It was a difficult day when he told the members of his band that he would not play for dances anymore. However, one of the musicians, a member of the church in which Michael was led to the Lord, convinced him that it would be all right to play again for dances; that way he could win some of the people to Christ.

ABOUT MIDNIGHT I laid aside my instrument and approached a friend. "Are you a Christian?" I asked.

"No. Are you?"

"Yes, I am," I said.

"Then what in the world are you doing here?"

I suddenly realized my mother must be right—I had no business being there. That night, still a new Christian, I walked away from a promising career, and right into the arms of a Savior waiting for my surrender with the reassurance of Jeremiah 29:11: " 'For I know the plans I have for you,' declares the LORD, 'plans to prosper you and not to harm you, plans to give you hope and a future' " (NIV).

I fell deeply in love with the Lord, and more than anything I wanted to talk to Him constantly. But every time I got down on my knees to pray, I thought of the dirty stories I told and heard while playing for burlesque shows. Oh, that almost drove me crazy. "How, Lord, can I overcome this?" He laid it on my heart to memorize Bible verses. So I wrote the verses on cards, and I carried some in every pocket. As I walked or rode, I memorized Bible verses. Like corks in a glass, as my heart became filled with the water of the word, the corks of dirty stories floated out, and my heart was cleansed.

These verses helped me to overcome other things too, like smoking and drinking. I wondered, "Is it wrong to smoke? To drink wine?" My father had given me more wine to drink than my mother gave me milk when I was growing up. He wanted me to learn to smoke an Italian cigar and drink Italian wine by the time I was five, and I did.

While thinking on these things, holding a glass of wine in one hand and a cigarette in the other, I thought of 1 Corinthians 10:31: "Whatever you do, do all to the glory of God." I wondered, "Lord, are You being glorified by my smoking and drinking?" It seemed I could hear Him answer no. I was constrained to turn from these things.

The faith of Michael's mother, always enhanced with kindness, blessed the five children in other ways. She turned obstacles into opportunities. She refused to be fettered by fears, defeated by dangers, or overcome by opposition. She taught the family that suffering is not an accident, but an apparatus. It is not an obstacle for a setback, but an opportunity for success. Suffering is not sent to destroy lives, but to develop them.

An old proverb says, "When fate throws a dagger at you, there are two ways you can catch it; by the blade or the handle." Mrs. Guido kept a handle on everything, and as she was submissive to the Lord she was strengthened. Her trust in Him for the conversion of her husband finally triumphed. Michael tells how it happened.

ALL THE TIME I was a student at Moody my father was heavy on my heart. More than life itself I wanted my father to become a

Christian. One day I was especially burdened for him. That night when I went to bed, I could not sleep. Jumping out of bed and dressing quickly, I hurried to the depot and boarded the Nickel Plate train for Lorain, praying all the way for my father's conversion.

Arriving early in the morning, I walked to our home, and Mother greeted me with alarm. "What's wrong?" she asked.

"I couldn't sleep," I replied. "I've been burdened for Pa."

"I've been deeply burdened too," she said, "but he's quite angry this morning, and he started drinking very early. I know you'll want to talk to him, but be careful. You know what he threatened to do to you if you ever brought up the matter of salvation. And remember, he's shaving with a straight razor." Running up the steps, I hurriedly knocked on the bathroom door. My father opened the door and, seeing it was me, sprang toward me with his razor. I reached out and hugged him as I said, "Pa, I don't care what you do to me. I only want you to be a Christian. Heaven would be awfully lonesome without you. You will receive Jesus, won't you?" Weeping, we knelt together, and my father received the Lord Jesus as his Savior.

What a joy it was to have my father join our family altar. He seldom prayed out loud, but as we prayed, he invariably sobbed. He was deeply moved by our devotion to our Lord and our love for him.

We prayed that our Lord would blot out from his remembrance how he used to curse us and thrash us for our faith, and our Lord did. Many times he asked, "Did I ever hurt you because you became a Christian?" I wasn't lying when I assured him that he had helped—for he really had. The persecution made me better, not bitter. It deepened my faith, increased my love for the Lord, and put iron in my soul. It prepared me for what would follow. How I thank God for it now.

There was a slow growth of grace in his life. There were times when I wept much in prayer because his faith wasn't always vocal and visual. I found help in turning to the Bible. Had I been with the Lord Jesus when He was praying in the garden and Judas came up and hugged Him and kissed Him, I might have said, "There's a Christian!" Had I been present when Peter cut off a man's ear, I might have asked, "Is he a Christian?" How much better it is to go by faith than by sight.

When Paul wrote, "Put on kindness," he did not mean a coat to be worn only part of the time. Kindness is the consistent evidence of the child of God. Mrs. Guido's paid eternal dividends.

Shortly before Michael's conversion, he heard a man sing, "My Father is rich." He sighed and thought, "If only He were my Father." And today He is!

Together, Michael and his mother helped the three sisters grow in the faith. Michael served as a model in his faithful church attendance, devotions, and actions. These talented and lovely girls grew eager to live and labor for the Lord. However, a dilemma developed for Michael. He wanted to go to college or seminary after he graduated from Moody Bible Institute. Acutely aware that his sisters should be away from home and receive Bible training, he still felt that he lacked education. He decided in favor of his sisters and paid their way through school.

In asking the Lord to make it possible to put them through Moody, he also prayed that God would allow him to work with God-honoring men—men who were filled with love and wisdom and who would help him grow in grace and a knowledge of the Lord. The prayer was heard!

He remembers, with a smile, being in a meeting with a pastor whom he admired. The pastor unexpectedly announced one evening that "Michael Guido has never told us his needs, and he never asks for money. But I happen to know that, although he's not married, he's putting his three *daughters* through Moody Bible Institute.

Everyone in the audience broke up with laughter and wonder. Michael was not sure what he had done wrong. Then a deacon arose to correct the pastor, telling him that it was Michael's sisters, not daughters, he was educating.

His adventure in faith for his sisters was worthy. Roxie became an outstanding gospel pianist. She traveled with him for some time, and the Lord used her mightily in meetings. One afternoon when they were on their way to a church revival in a southern city, they saw some men moving a piano out of a music store and onto a truck. With a twinkle in her eye, Roxie asked, "Know what I'm thinking?"

His knowing glance mirrored his answer, "I'm afraid I do, but go ahead!"

Roxie went to the piano movers and said, "Hold up a minute." With that, she lifted the cover of the piano and started playing beautifully. A crowd soon gathered. Michael started singing. After a couple of minutes, he brought a one-minute message. The people responded to the extemporaneous concert, and many came to the meeting that evening.

When Roxie married, she settled in Kentucky and became pianist and choir director for various churches in Kentucky and Indiana.

Tonie became a fine cellist, vocal soloist, and song leader. She loved telling Bible stories and perfected her winsome method. She married a Moody student who pastored churches in Louisiana and was true to the Lord.

Margie graduated from Moody and also married a Moody student and settled in her hometown. She helped her mother with children's Bible classes and kept the faith.

All three sisters are in heaven today, having blessed many during their lifetimes.

Because of their age difference, Larry, the youngest brother, was more like a son than a brother to Michael. One night when Michael was preaching in Lorain, the family's hometown, he asked the people at the service to bow their heads and open the doors of their hearts to receive Jesus as Savior. Five-year-old Larry raised his hand. Michael, not noticing his little brother, extended the invitation, "Isn't anyone there?"

"What about me? I want to receive Jesus." That night was Larry's spiritual birth. What joy it was to his mother's heart and to a brother who was sowing gospel seeds.

One day Michael came home after conducting a series of evangelistic meetings and told his mother of the exciting experiences he had enjoyed. Weeping, she said, "I wish I wasn't tied down. I wish I could go out and reach and teach others the Word."

He answered, "Mother, that's exactly what you're doing. You taught me; you're teaching your three girls and one other son. You're teaching them now for God. And you will be reaching millions through us."

Ma was reminded of a story of a brilliant writer who married and whom God blessed with a family. One day an old college friend said to her, "It's a pity you gave up writing books."

"I haven't given up writing books," she answered. "I've written two."

"What are their titles?" asked the friend.

She replied, "Ethel and Albert. Those are my two children. I'm writing living epistles known and read of all men that they have been with Jesus."

Julia Guido knew that a mother cannot change the color of her child's eyes, but she can help give the eyes sympathy, not scorn; kindness, not cruelty. A mother cannot change the features of her child, but she can help give the face hopefulness, not hopelessness; helpfulness, not hurtfulness. A mother cannot change her child's comeliness, but she can help a countenance register affection, not aggression; awareness, not anxiety.

She had been frail for many years. The family worried about her weak heart and the complications from it. She felt concern for young Larry. Michael and his wife pledged to care for and educate Larry. Through the years and after her death, they supported him in faith and education. Through a high school academy, university, and two seminaries, Larry has been an outstanding scholar.

He became a chaplain in the United States Navy,

earned a doctorate in philosophy, and had a fine career as a college professor. In later years he supervised the Clint Eastwood Youth Program in Monterey, California, and he was associated with a family advocacy program at Fort Ord, California, in the naval post-graduate school.

Michael takes deserved pride in his brother's and sisters' schooling. His unselfishness, learned from his mother, will find its reward in heaven. Today, only Michael and Larry survive, but imbedded in their hearts and lives are Ma's strength and kindness, the willingness to overcome the odds against Pa's success as an immigrant to America, and the consistent joy the years have brought. Faith and prayer were her children's foundation, and the "foundations of God stand sure."

An old Italian prayer summarizes Julia Guido. In the midst of problems or persecution she rested on God's promises and said, "*Signore, ti ringrazio per il giorno che mi hai datto* (Lord, I thank You for the day You have given me)."

Each morning she sowed her seeds of kindness with prayer. And she continued into the noontide and deep into the night.

CHAPTER 3

SOWING IN THE NOONTIDE

Oh, magnify the LORD with me,
And let us exalt His name together.

Psalm 34:3

When Michael Guido graduated from Moody, he had twenty-five dollars left in his pocket. He wondered why. Having lived by faith and total dependence on the Lord, he was amazed at this excess. After arriving at home, he experienced trouble with his throat. The results of the examination caused the doctor to burst into song, "The Yanks are coming." He went on to explain that Michael's tonsils had to be removed. The cost of the surgery? Twenty-five dollars.

"Thank you, Lord!" exclaimed the former student. "Before I called, You answered."

Because of the strain placed on the throat in all the street meetings, singing and evangelistic endeavors, it was suggested that Michael spend some time in Florida. How kind of the Lord to have provided the way through Miss Eddy of the Extension Department at Moody.

Miss Eddy had called him prior to graduation stating, "Michael, I recommended you to my favorite preacher, W. W. Shannon. He needs an assistant, one who can sing and lead singing and who can work with young people."

He desires a man who has a passion for souls. I gave him your name. He will call you today or tomorrow."

Michael tells these experiences best—experiences that, in God's time, led this sower to his lady!

HE DID CALL and hired me sight unseen! He told me that he would send a train ticket and expected me in two weeks.

"Lord willing," I said, "I'll be there."

"I'll meet you at the station," he promised.

But the train ran late, so Mr. Shannon left. Before he returned, I had arrived in Sebring. Looking around for someone to lead to the Lord, I was drawn to an employee of the railroad. I talked to him about the Lord and read to him from the Word; then together we knelt while he called upon the name of the Lord.

Mr. Shannon drove up while we were praying. When we rose from our knees, he started to cry. "Son," he said, "I've been here for several years, and I never talked to that man about his salvation. You come, and in a few minutes you lead him to the Lord. I am ashamed of myself. You see, I came here to retire. The fishing is good. The church is small. I was taking it easy. But from now on I'm going to do more for the Lord and the lost."

Burdened for the lost, I immediately started calling on each officer and teacher of the First Presbyterian Church to see what I could do to be profitable to Christ and the church. I found some unsaved, others unsure of their salvation, but many who loved the Lord. Together we started out to lead the lost to the Lord, beginning with the leaders.

One night a deacon drove me to a political meeting where I was to speak. I urged the men to believe and behave the gospel. Many were moved. Some met with me after the meeting and turned their lives over to the Lord. The deacon drove me to the hotel, and before I got out of his car, I suggested we pray.

"In an automobile?" he asked.

"Yes," I answered. "I'd rather pray in your car than in the belly of a fish as Jonah did."

"Well," he said, "go ahead."

I prayed, "Lord Jesus, be pleased to bless the message and save the mayor and the councilmen and . . ."

Just then this deacon poked me in the ribs and asked, "Why don't you ask the Lord to save me?"

"You? A deacon and a Sunday school superintendent?"

"Yes," he said. "Ask God to save me. I am a church member, but I have never been converted."

I prayed for him, and there in his car, this businessman, Joe M. Stiles, Sr., received Jesus as his Lord and Savior. He went on to grow in grace, and the Lord richly blessed him in his witnessing and working. Later Joe became a member of the Guido Evangelistic Association Board of Directors, helping us wonderfully in this work of our Lord.

Pastor Shannon was a man's man, and he taught me much. Before his conversion he managed a brewery, owned a liquor store, and was the mayor of his hometown, Berwick, Pennsylvania. Because of his connection with the town newspaper, Bill Shannon went to interview an evangelist who had come to conduct a citywide revival. After introducing himself, Shannon started asking questions.

"Sir," the evangelist told him, "you don't need to know anything about me. But you do need to know my Savior."

Amazed at the man's humility and interest in his salvation, Shannon stayed to hear him preach. When the invitation was given, he went forward and received the Lord Jesus as his Savior.

His father, an old Methodist class leader, hugged him and said, "Let's go home and tell your mom."

Walking into his mother's bedroom, the forty-year-old politician said, "Guess what, Mom."

"I know, son," she interrupted. "You got converted."

"How do you know? Did someone tell you?" he asked.

"No," she replied, "but I've been praying for your conversion every day for forty years."

Mr. Shannon gave up his liquor business and set out to make restitution. He moved out of his beautiful home, and into a rundown house on a back street. He advertised in the paper that if he owed anyone anything, he would settle on their terms. Satisfying those demands, paying off all his debts, and getting victory over alcoholism, Mr. Shannon felt led of the Lord to give himself for full-time Christian work.

Following a successful career as an advance man for the evangelist who had led him to the Lord, Mr. Shannon became an evangelist for the Moody Bible Institute. Feeling the need for a warmer climate and having been urged to slow down, he accepted the pastorate of the First Presbyterian Church. How happy I am the Lord led him to invite me to become his assistant and director of music. He was like a father to me.

Having played nightclubs, my flashy dress was a bit much for the dear folk at the Presbyterian church. They toned down my wardrobe, taught me to dress more sedately, and helped me a great deal. Many of the members became the dearest and sweetest friends I have ever enjoyed.

But there were a few who did not appreciate my bringing some of the converts into the church—the alcoholics, addicts, prostitutes, and some of the basest sort who came to the Lord—whom I invited to the services and to sing in the choir. These few felt I was breaking up their country-club society by introducing this rough element into their midst.

We formed the S.O.S. (Save Other Souls) Club and had a very fruitful ministry. We met one night a week, prayed for the lost, then selected one or two on whom to concentrate. The next day the S.O.S. members called on those selected, and invariably, before the week was over, they were led, through the gracious Holy Spirit, to the Lord. Those converts then joined the club. We were bound by the tie of His true love. If one had a pain, everyone felt it.

This soul-winning activity revived the pastor, and Mr. Shannon resigned his pastorate to become an evangelist with Moody. The church asked me to continue with them. It was a thrilling experience to search the Scriptures daily, to pray unceasingly, and to serve sacrificially.

Our S.O.S. Club grew and became more fruitful. When one rejoiced, everyone rejoiced. Each one of us grew in grace.

One thing that led us to pray more and to work harder was the burden the Lord placed on our hearts for the people of our city and county. Sebring was a tourist city that boasted renowned hotels for the rich and famous. Every Sunday night after the evening service, I was invited to the leading hotel to sing and speak to the tourists. After some congregational singing, accompanied by the hotel orchestra, I was allowed to bring a message, and a goodly number of tourists opened the door of their hearts to the Lord. What thrilling results we experienced.

But the devil stirred up opposition in the church. Many times at night I packed my bags to leave and unpacked them again in the morning. This put more iron into my soul, tenderized my forbearance, and brought me closer to the Lord. I am thankful for those growing experiences.

One day I was informed that a trial was to be held in our church. Officials came from headquarters to investigate what had been reported as "disorder in worship," by those who did not appreciate what I was doing. I do not blame them—I'm still surprised the Lord loves me. And it was true! I had brought converts who had lived wicked lives and who had indulged in the more sordid, "dirtier" sins into the church.

At the proceedings, the converts heard the charges and started popping up, like popcorn, all over the congregation, telling of their conversion. This unplanned demonstration went on uninterrupted for a time before the denomination official finally said, "If this is disorder in worship, may the Lord send it to each one of our churches. This meeting is dismissed."

Mr. Shannon began to experience thrilling meetings, and he invited me to join him. Many of the townspeople wanted me to stay. The businessmen offered to pay my salary, and the Sebring Hotel offered to entertain me free of charge if I would stay and work with the young people. But my heart stood tall for evangelism, and the Lord led me to rejoin W. W. Shannon as his song leader.

The Lord blessed our meetings, and I was grateful for the lessons I learned by watching him and working with him. He taught me how to organize, advertise, and agonize.

Many times I found him crying in his motel room. "Preacher," I asked, "what is wrong? Is there anything I can do to help?"

"No," he replied, "I am crying because of the years I wasted before I gave my life to the Lord. Think of it—forty years old before I was saved. I ruined my body with drink. But I know the Lord has forgiven me."

One of Mr. Shannon's closest friends was Dr. Harry McCormick Lintz, a popular and powerful preacher who pastored the thriving First Baptist Church of Lake Charles, Louisiana. Dr. Lintz needed an associate to sing, direct the choir, and work with young people. With Mr. Shannon's consent, Dr. Lintz approached me. After the interview and much prayer for God's guidance, I felt led to leave Mr. Shannon and join Dr. Lintz.

Dr. Lintz was a polished preacher. He loved the Lord and he lived His Word. Serving as his associate, I learned much. Those were great days. The Lord blessed with an average of ten additions every Sunday for fifty-two Sundays.

One day Dr. Lintz suggested that I be ordained. Oh, I was honored, and I prepared for the ordination. Dr. Lintz told me to be "prayed up and filled up with the Holy Spirit and to be ready to give a Bible verse for every answer to their questions."

One of the questions was "Are you a premillennialist or a postmillennialist?" I am a premillennialist. I was aware there were many on the questioning council who wanted to know why. So I answered, "I can't find the words *premillennialist* or *postmillennialist* in the Bible."

Then they came to the matter of Communion. One asked, "Do you believe in closed communion?"

"Sir," I replied, "I don't remember finding that expression in the Bible." Pleased with the answers, they ordained me. I was so grateful to God for Dr. Lintz and the pastors on the ordination committee.

My time with Dr. Lintz was pleasurable and profitable. I will always be indebted to him for everything he taught me, by lip and by life. But Mr. Shannon once again needed me as he was getting up in years. Dr. Lintz, Mr. Shannon, and I prayed much about this, and I felt led to return to Mr. Shannon.

THE SOWER DISCOVERS HIS LADY

Mr. Shannon was still an evangelist for the Moody Bible Institute when I rejoined him, and we enjoyed the Lord's blessing upon our crusades. Over and over he said to me, "Michael, before the Lord calls me home to heaven, I hope He will allow me to meet the one He chooses to be your wife. I know He has a choice person for you." Daily, when we prayed together, he voiced this petition to the Lord. The Lord started working in my heart and in the heart of a lovely young lady.

On the arrival of a new schedule, we learned that Moody had booked us for a revival with the Reverend and Mrs. C. K. Everett of the First Baptist Church in Metter, Georgia, a town with a population of fewer than three thousand.

The Everetts were at Moody when I was a student, and I loved them. But I did not like small towns, so I tried to get out of going to Metter. Mr. Shannon and Mr. Everett would not let me. The Lord blessed with crowds and conversions. It was a real revival, one of the greatest of our lives.

I was invited to go to the high school and speak to the students every day. On the very first day, the superintendent said to me, "We have a beautiful and talented teacher I want you to meet and talk to about the Lord. She graduated from college very young, finished her premed, and has won a scholarship to Johns Hopkins to study medicine, but she's an agnostic. I'm praying that you will lead her to the Lord."

Just then the teacher walked down the hall. "Miss Forehand," he said, "I want you to meet this preacher."

"I don't want to meet any preacher," she replied, and she kept on walking.

Catching up with her, I asked, "Won't you please come to our revival?"

"No, sir," she stated emphatically.

"Why won't you?"

"There is no God," she replied.

Opening my Bible to Psalm 14:1, I politely asked her to read the verse aloud.

She read, "The fool has said in his heart, 'There is no God.'" Looking angrily at me she said, "You're calling me a fool."

"No, ma'am," I answered, "God beat me to it." In a rage, she left me.

She was the leader of the Victory Corps, a band of patriotic juniors and seniors, engaged in calisthenics and drills. Feeling they needed the practice and discipline of marching into buildings, she marched them into the church for the morning meetings. Enjoying those, Audrey returned in the evening and found the services refreshing. One night some of the leaders invited Mr. Shannon and me for ice cream and Georgia peaches. By design, they included Audrey.

Not wanting her to walk home alone, I accompanied her. To my horror, her mother met me at the door with a shotgun! Some tough, incorrigible prisoners who had escaped from the state prison in Reidsville, about thirty miles away, had been seen in Metter, and Audrey's mother was prepared for them. However, I wasn't prepared to be introduced to someone holding a shotgun.

I found her parents to be two of the kindest, sweetest, finest people I had ever met. How much I enjoyed her father's humor and her mother's sweetness. Today we smile about a "shotgun" intro to our wedding.

Day after day and night after night I talked with Audrey about the Lord. Every time she gave me an argument, I responded with a Bible verse. I was no match for her brilliant arguments, but the Bible was just what she needed. Slowly her heart became softer, her arguments became fewer, and at last I had the supreme honor of leading Audrey to the Lord.

Immediately after the Metter meeting, Mr. Shannon and I left for Chicago, but I could not get Audrey off my mind. Wanting her to grow in grace, I sent her a beautiful leather New Testament and later a most beautiful Bible. Each time she sent her heartfelt appreciation by return mail. Her pastor, C. K. Everett, kept me posted on her growth in grace, her public confession, and her baptism.

Audrey's first big test came a few weeks later when she received an invitation to lead the Naval Academy Ball. This was a high honor. They offered to pay her travel expenses and a chaperone and to buy her clothes. Without any hesitation, she felt she could not accept the invitation to the glory of God. She turned it down. I was thrilled when her pastor told me about it, and I wrote to her expressing my joy. She replied, expressing her love for the Lord. I found myself falling in love—she was unlike any woman I had ever met.

When we saw that we would be drawn into the Second World

War, Mr. Shannon and I went to Washington and met with some of our outstanding Christian representatives and senators and asked for a special permit to go onto the military bases to preach the gospel and distribute New Testaments. Prepared with letters from appropriate offices, we contacted the Pocket Testament of Philadelphia and worked out an arrangement with Moody Bible Institute to give out the Word of the Lord to service personnel.

Our ministry was nationwide, but every time Mr. Shannon asked where we should go next, I would always answer, "I feel led to go to Georgia." With a twinkle in his eye, he would agree.

I called Audrey one day and asked her if I could come see her. Thrilled, she said, "Please do."

Pastor Everett and his wife invited me to stay with them, so I left immediately. About fifteen miles from Metter, I was recognized by a farmer as I passed his field. He hurried inside and phoned Audrey that I was on my way. A little farther along, another farmer saw me, and he added his report. I was recognized several more times on the way into town, and each time, Audrey was duly apprised of my progress so that when I finally arrived, she was waiting for me outside. So much for surprising her—but I began to learn about the inner workings of a small town.

One day while I was visiting with the pastor, I realized I was going to be late for a date I had made with Audrey. I eagerly accepted the loan of a bicycle, jumped on it, and started to pedal. Just then it dawned on me that I had never ridden a bicycle before—we had never had one when I was a kid—and here I was riding one for the first time. Thinking about it frightened me a little; I took a tumble and landed right in front of Audrey. Looking up at her I said, "Well, you can sure say I fell for you."

Whenever there was any free time between meetings, I headed for the Everetts' in Metter so I could date Audrey. We were deeply in love with one another. During one of our crusades, I decided to propose. I knew, deep within my heart, she was God's choice for me, and believing that she would accept, I bought a diamond ring with the biggest check I had ever written.

Audrey remembers three wonderful months of correspondence and Michael's brief visits, infrequent because the war made traveling difficult. Then Michael wrote and asked her to travel to Florida, where he was going to hold a revival meeting.

In those days girls in the South did not venture out alone or unchaperoned. Although Michael had assured her that she could stay with the Shannons, her mother refused to consider it until Audrey had received a *personal* invitation from them. Mrs. Shannon obliged by formally inviting Audrey to be a guest in their home, instructing her to travel by train. This still did not solve the problem of traveling alone, so the Shannons rerouted their trip from Pennsylvania to Florida through Metter, and Audrey made the journey with them. Although a college graduate and employed, she still acceded to the wishes of her folks.

Her Florida visit lasted for a week. It was a joyous time to be with Michael.

ONE DAY THE pastor of the church where I was conducting the meetings told me a woman who wanted to become a Christian had called, asking that I go see her. When I asked him to accompany me, he said that he couldn't—he had another appointment. I never called alone on women, so I asked Audrey to go with me. She was thrilled.

We went to the address and walked up the front steps, where I rang the doorbell. I suddenly had an urge to step back, leaving Audrey at the door. When it opened, a pregnant girl rushed out to embrace the unsuspecting young preacher, but she gathered Audrey into her arms instead as flashbulbs popped.

She finally confessed, "I'm pregnant. You're a good-looking man. You dress well. I thought I could frame you and force you to marry me—or at least support my child."

How grateful I was for Audrey. She seemed to know what to do in every emergency, and she always did the right and beautiful thing. More and more I knew she was the one for me.

SECOND TO NONE

Audrey was very aware when she decided to marry Michael that two things in their lives would never change:

She would always be second to the ministry, and Michael would never retire.

When these two special people became one, there was never the question of which one. They complemented each other in every way. As for being second, she is *second to none* and there are no signs of retirement for the Guidos.

Audrey is convinced God trained her for her part in this ministry:

MY MOTHER AND father were sharecroppers, as was Dad's father before him. Mother's family was more prosperous, owning many acres of farmland and a nice country home. However, my dad was very conservative and a very hard worker. A year after they were married, I was born. In three years they had worked and saved enough money to buy a lot and build a house in town. Dad was a carpenter and built the house himself. He also built a little general store that Mother began to operate. They sold groceries, gasoline, and kerosene. I learned to make change and pump gasoline before I began school at the age of six. When I was five, my sister was born. Dad was now doing carpentry, brick-laying, and other jobs while Mother managed the store that we continued to operate until I left for college. Mother and Dad worked hard to see that my sister Ailene and I could have the advantages they never had.

Through the years, Dad worked for Standard Oil Company and bought some farmland. The income from the store provided our groceries, living expenses, and eventually college expenses. Times in the twenties and thirties were difficult. My parents fed many families during those hard years.

Mother and Dad were wonderful, loving, caring people. They set a good example for us. Though they, especially Dad, were not active in church work until later, the standards and morals they instilled in my sister and me were very high.

During the seventh grade, at age thirteen, I contracted typhoid fever. I was out of school for about half of that year but managed to keep up with my class through the help of teachers and my family. The illness left me with a problem with my ankles, which later required leg braces. I was unable to walk the mile to school, so Mother and Dad got a '29 Chevrolet to drive me. It was fun, even with the handicap. Five years later, I walked into the doctor's office, free of braces, and determined to be a physician.

> At Georgia State College for Women in Milledgeville, she stayed on the dean's list. Her parents wanted her to teach rather than practice medicine, so she took education courses along with premed. She earned a coveted medical scholarship from Johns Hopkins University. Her love for chemistry and physics later impacted their ministry, and her preciseness also contributed to making the Metter ministry a model for secular and Christian organizations.
>
> While Audrey was with the Shannons, Michael wrote her parents that he intended to ask her to marry him and that he sincerely hoped they would approve. While her parents gave their blessing, there was a wonderful black woman, with the family since Audrey was a child, who severely disapproved. She felt she could never accept that "Yankee" preacher who would take her Audrey away forever. Once back in Metter, Michael won the woman's heart, and Aunt Hannah became one of his best boosters.
>
> One afternoon Mrs. Shannon asked Audrey's help in preparing dinner for a friend invited after the evening service. Audrey spent most of the afternoon frying chicken. Michael arrived, insisting that she come with him at once. Audrey was reluctant to leave, but being a good sport, she took off her apron and followed him out. Perfumed with the fragrance of the oil of frying chicken, Audrey accepted the diamond ring Michael offered. They were both overjoyed. Then she realized that the meal she had prepared inside was for their engagement announcement. Everyone was in on the secret except Audrey. How she loved the surprise!

AUDREY HAD BEEN given a scholarship to Johns Hopkins to study medicine, and I knew that once she started something, she would complete it. So I did what I had to do quickly. Knowing that her parents' anniversary was Thanksgiving Day that year, I suggested that we get married then. She agreed, believing that it would be better to pass out the gospel than prescription pills.

The date was set, but by that time I, too, was on the Moody staff, and Mr. Shannon and I had been booked for a meeting in Emporia, Kansas, which could not be canceled. It was impossible for me to get to Metter for the wedding, so I asked Audrey to come to Lorain and be married in our home. Bless her heart, she said she would.

I told my mother that we would be married on Thanksgiving Day in Lorain, and she said, "Son, don't you think you ought to put this off for a while?"

"Ma," I reminded her, "I'm twenty-nine. The Lord Jesus said, 'What you do, do quickly.'"

"Yes," she agreed, "and Judas hanged himself. I know you are marrying God's choice, and from what you say she must be wonderful. I'm happy for you."

I met Audrey, who had never traveled on a train before, in Cleveland, and together we made the journey to Lorain. I got off the train first and turned to help Audrey off. Suddenly I felt the firm grip of two hands on my shoulders, holding me so that I could not move. I could see from his coat I was in the grip of an officer of the law. He said angrily, "You louse! I've been searching for you through five states. At last I've caught up with you. You're under arrest for bigamy; hold out your hands for the cuffs."

Audrey turned red and nearly fainted. I did not know what to think. When I turned around I discovered my uncle, playing one of his practical jokes on us. But what a devastating one!

My uncle then drove us to the house where my mother, father, sisters, brother, and all the aunts and uncles had gathered to give us a warm greeting. She fell in love with the family, and they with her. They found her to be kind, sweet, and helpful.

While mother prepared a seven-course Italian dinner, Larry and I cooked up some awful tricks. We put a false bottom on Audrey's chair; when she sat down, it made a horrible noise. She picked up her water glass and the coaster came up with it. She unfolded her napkin and a cap exploded. She picked up a spoon—it collapsed. She started to sip her coffee—the saucer was stuck to the cup. What a dinner! She endeared herself to the whole family by laughing heartily with us. They exclaimed that nothing was too good for her.

Mr. Shannon performed the ceremony; Noel O. Lyons, director of the extension staff at Moody, was best man; Cornelius Brown, the man who had led me into singing, played the piano as we were married.

Audrey was to come down our beautiful spiral staircase, where I was waiting to receive her. She was extraordinarily lovely. A sweet hush fell over the guests. Just as I joined Audrey, Mr. Brown, modulating from one song to another, eased into a few bars of "Jesus, I My Cross Have Taken." I thought some of us would double up with laughter. During the ceremony, Larry blurted out, "I don't have a brother anymore." In all her bridal dignity, Audrey assured him that he not only had a brother, but another sister as well.

Then that rascally brother of mine played a trick on me. A young lady from one of the churches where I had served had sent me a picture of herself. I thought I had thrown it out, but Larry found it and put it in my suitcase. Imagine my horror when we opened the suitcase on our wedding night and found another girl's picture in it. That was a "Kodak moment" I want to forget.

Our five o'clock wedding was followed by another exciting Italian dinner my mother had prepared. After dinner the preacher, the best man, Audrey, and I boarded the train for Chicago.

We had a sleeping car, and presently the other two in our party knocked on the door and advised us not to go to bed until we had all gathered for a time of Bible reading and prayer. I tried to convince her that they were teasing, but not having been around preachers much before, Audrey thought they were serious and waited a long time for those two to come in. They did not.

The best man persuaded my brother to give him a tube of

toothpaste. In some way they managed to substitute some fiery ointment rub for some of the toothpaste and that night Audrey received the "hottest kiss I ever had."

We hurried to Moody upon our arrival in Chicago, anxious that everyone get acquainted. Noel Lyons introduced Audrey who, being the cut-up he was, proceeded to dance a jig—just as Dr. Houghton, the president of the Institute, walked up. There were some red faces and a lot of laughter.

Then Audrey met the rest of the staff and faced their scrutiny. She used cosmetics becomingly, but some of the workers in our department disapproved. I quickly defended her by pointing out that I wanted her to, and I reminded them of the words of Dr. Harry Ironside, famous pastor of the Moody Memorial Church: "Paint makes any building look good."

Several coworkers cornered Audrey and asked her if she could sing or play the piano. "No," she replied, "I don't know a note from a mortgage."

Turning to me, one inquired, "Then why did you marry her?"

"Because I love her," was my enthusiastic answer.

It hurt Audrey that she could not sing with me or accompany me, but I assured her that I loved her and wanted God's mate for me, not a musician. She was His helpmate for me. I could never have found a better one.

The Guidos' first trip, after a Kansas honeymoon, was to a revival. It was the beginning of a twenty-year traveling schedule marked with miracles and blessings, discouragements, and disasters, but never with defeat. Each moment was a time to practice the presence of God and realize they were not just conquerors, but *more* than conquerors through Him that loved them both so much.

It may still surprise people in the nineties that leaders are born women! Behind every great woman is usually a group of surprised men. Yet through the years, business professionals have lauded Audrey's acumen, and in 1982 she received a prestigious Woman of Achievement award from the Business Women's Club in appreciation for her exceptional leadership and integrity.

She possesses both sense and sensibility and manages not with a stern finger, but with an inner commitment to excellence.

States her adoring husband,

AUDREY IS SO integral to the work. I appreciate her. She is special. She is a great woman and an encouragement to me and others. Not too many wives want to stay in the background. Audrey is happily content there just so someone else might come to know the Lord. I often say she is the brains of this work. She cares for the finances, the staff, and the purchasing, all in a gracious manner. She organizes and specializes in quality. How often I have tried to push her a bit more to the front. No, she lovingly shies away. Hid with Christ, in God, for His service and my blessing.

From a consensus of people who know her, Audrey is best defined as having perfected the gentle art of being there. Ready to serve, to sow and spread more seeds in the background of her husband, she emulates the good wife of Proverbs 31:

> Who can find a virtuous wife?
> For her worth is far above rubies.
> The heart of her husband safely trusts her. . . .
> She girds herself with strength. . . .
> And her lamp does not go out by night. . . .
> Strength and honor are her clothing;
> She shall rejoice in time to come. . . .
> She watches over the ways of her household,
> And does not eat the bread of idleness.
> Her [spiritual] children rise up and call her
>   blessed;
> Her husband also, and he praises her;
> "Many daughters have done well,
> But you excel them all" (10–11, 17, 18, 25, 27–29).

That is Audrey. She has never surrendered to mediocrity. She possesses a beautiful smile and a resilient heart. She is a twenty-first-century executive who knows her work for the Lord will last forever.

CHAPTER 4

WAITING FOR THE HARVEST

Jesus said to them, "My food is to do the will of Him who sent Me, and to finish His work. . . . Behold, I say to you, lift up your eyes and look at the fields, for they are already white for harvest! . . . He who reaps receives wages and gathers fruit for eternal life, that both he who sows and he who reaps may rejoice together.

John 4:34–36

As Michael walked down River Street in Savannah, a little boy shouted, "Hey, Mom! There's the Jesus commercial man!" Such recognition came from over thirty years of scattering seeds of faith to the world. Michael is called "the Sower," "the Minute-Message-Man," or "the preacher who cares for the prostitutes and perfectionists, the down and out, and the up and out." A common denominator runs through the various titles:

He sows a good seed!

Michael's distinct message is introduced by the sound of twittering birds and moves quickly to an inventive presentation of the gospel message that is the "seed for the garden of your heart." He makes no direct requests for money and could never be accused of being in broadcast evangelism for earthly gain. Truly the wage he receives is the gathered fruit for life eternal.

The messages are carried between commercials of well-known talk shows, during NFL games, and once during a break from a presidential inauguration. The statistics are impressive: daily telecasts on more than 500 stations, with an undetermined number of airings; three thousand cable systems; and three hundred radio stations that broadcast up to four programs a day. KAAY, Little Rock, Arkansas, a 50,000-watt station covering thirteen foreign countries and twenty-seven states, transmits the one-minute broadcast ten times a day. HCJB, Quito, Ecuador, penetrates all seven continents and airs two programs: the fifteen-minute and the one-minute. Far East Broadcasting covers two-thirds of the globe. A safe, conservative estimate is that more than three thousand programs are aired each week. In addition, fifteen hundred newspapers publish Michael's column, and Dial-A-Prayer answers uncounted calls.

Listeners, media personnel, and the more than one thousand people who come to the headquarters of the Sower each month ask the same question. However the question is framed, they all want to know, how did all this start? Michael's answer is always the same:

FOR TWENTY YEARS we were "on the road again"—and again. I traveled with evangelists, pastored a church, and was an evangelist myself. Audrey was the perfect companion for me. She used her chemistry knowledge to create demonstrations that illustrated Bible truths. And she became an accomplished magician! Her programs and antics startled and stunned our auditorium crowds. And those crowds remembered her spiritual applications.

Once the Lord and thrifty Audrey made it possible for us to save enough money in 1957 to buy a small mobile home, which would provide a place to take a break from our busy schedule.

On one occasion we had planned to rest for a month, but a pastor in Atlanta called and asked us to come for a special meeting. We prayed about his request and felt led to go. It seemed to be a wonderful opportunity with a bonus: we would be able to spend some time with my "baby" brother Larry, who just two days before had become the minister of education at the First Baptist Church of Avondale Estates. We needed a car for the trip and were able to buy one from a gracious dealer in Tupelo, Mississippi. So travel to the meeting was fun, riding smoothly along in our new automobile.

As we neared Atlanta, we wondered what awaited us there. We hoped to be instruments of God's peace and forgiveness. We longed for revival. Audrey began reviewing her magic demonstration, hoping it would attract a crowd and prepare the people for my message.

At an intersection near Covington, Georgia, I slowed, noticed that there were stop signs for opposing traffic, and started cautiously across. Suddenly I felt a devastating jolt on the right side of the car. The blow hammered the new car, tearing, twisting, and wrenching the metal. Both vehicles were demolished.

When I came to, I couldn't find Audrey. I ran all around the car, but she wasn't there. No one was injured in the other car, but I was becoming frantic. I saw a trail of blood leading to a ditch—and then I saw Audrey. The force had ripped her clothes from her body, and she was lying in a pool of blood, her face cut from the forehead down to her chin. Her teeth had been damaged. Her hands, knees, and ankles were terribly bruised. And she could not see. When she regained conciousness, she asked if anyone else was hurt.

"Only you," I whispered, holding back a flood of tears.

An ambulance rushed her to a hospital in a nearby small town.

"Poor girl," said the doctor. "We can't do much for her here. Transfer her to Baptist Hospital in Atlanta, and we'll alert bone specialists, eye specialists, plastic surgeons, and others that you're on the way. Let's hurry her there."

We sped madly to Atlanta and committed Audrey to the Lord and the doctors' skill.

Four hours after the accident, Audrey's mother, sister, and brother-in-law arrived at the Atlanta hospital. They were shocked by her critical condition and mangled appearance. The doctor told them she might be blind and paralyzed—if she lived!

When Mrs. Forehand found me, visibly limping as I paced

the long, white halls, trickles of blood were dripping from my head down onto my torn clothes. She went for a doctor to examine me; I had a fractured ankle and three broken ribs. In my concern for Audrey, I was oblivious to my own injuries.

Mirrors were kept away from Audrey for the next several months while the plastic surgeon performed several reconstructive surgeries. Because of the severe injuries to her hands, the orthopedists said her days of magic were over.

Yet there were blessings from the apparent disaster. For years Audrey had suffered severe headaches from pressure caused by the pivot of the skull leading to the first vertebra. It was an inoperable condition. The sudden jolt was a healing one for that problem.

The Lord blessed the doctors with His wisdom for their minds; His skill for their hands; His love for their hearts. The day finally came when Audrey was released. It was a miracle!

An ambulance took her home to Metter. Face covered with bandages and body aching, she was still terribly crippled, but how we thanked the Lord for His marvelous mercy in sparing her life.

REDOUBLING OF EFFORTS

Not once did we ask, "Why, Lord?" Instead, we prayed, "What, Lord? What wilt Thou have us do?"

After traveling a while in silence I said, "Dear, the Lord spared our lives. Let's promise Him we will do the work of four people instead of two."

"That's a good idea," she responded softly.

"Let's ask the Lord to put on our hearts what He wants us to do," I said. We rode down the highway, praying silently, and then I asked, "Did the Lord tell you, dear?"

"He did," she said, "but you are going to laugh."

"Try me," I replied.

"The Lord laid a radio ministry on my heart," she answered.

"On mine too!" I exclaimed.

"What shall we name the program?" she wondered.

I closed my eyes, and all I could think of was Millet's painting of *The Sower,* which had made such an impact on my heart when I walked up those stairs at Crowell Hall on my first day at Moody Bible Institute. "We'll call it *The Sower,*" I said. "And for the theme song we'll use 'Bringing in the Sheaves.' We'll ask Ralph Carmichael to orchestrate it."

"Great," she agreed.

"But," I added, "we will never ask for money."

"Right," she responded. "We will make no plea for money over the air, in person, or by mail. And we'll never sell anything nor give anything away to get a mailing list to bleed for money."

"Yes," I said. "We'll claim Matthew 6:33: 'Seek first the kingdom of God and His righteousness, and all these things shall be added to you.'"

We've kept our promise and the Lord kept His. All we have needed the Lord has provided, and we have never asked any person for anything.

While we were holding an evangelistic meeting in Downers Grove, Illinois, a carpenter came to the Lord. One of his sons, Bob, a druggist, had come to the Lord in a previous meeting. And the Lord did a work of grace in the other son, Bill, a car salesman. Bill and his wife, Evie, became very dear friends. One day while talking with them about the radio ministry, we told them we had purchased turntables, tape recorders, and albums for broadcasting, but we needed a portable studio. Bill's carpenter father built one that resembled a telephone booth for us. Then we left for a revival in Tulare, California.

During the meeting we asked Ralph Carmichael to orchestrate our opening and closing theme song. He agreed happily, but when he gave us the price, we dropped to our knees to ask our Lord for the money. While we were praying, the phone rang.

"My name is Dr. R. P. Quackenbush," said the voice on the other end, "and I live in Paw Paw, Illinois. The Lord has laid it on my heart that you should start a broadcast. I just mailed you two thousand dollars."

I started crying, "That's just what we have been praying for—money for our broadcast."

We phoned Ralph Carmichael and told him the Lord had sent the money, and he invited us to come to Hollywood and be present for the recording. It was so exciting to be present as he orchestrated and directed a thrilling opening and closing for our proposed fifteen-minute broadcast of *The Sower.*

Then we went to a studio to record our first broadcasts. The engineer was drunk—his office manager said he was "lit up"— and told Audrey that he was too drunk to do a good job, but he would show her which buttons to push, how to ride the meters, cue the records, and work the turntables. He promised we would have good programs if she followed his instructions. And we did! Audrey was an apt student. After making fifty programs with him, she went on to engineer all of the programs for our broadcasts.

When we went into churches to conduct our evangelistic meetings, driving a station wagon and pulling a utility trailer, we brought the recording equipment and all our magic, an art Audrey continued to perfect to assist the evangelistic ministry. In one meeting a precious couple, the Reverend and Mrs. Stanley Welch, came to see us while we were recording. I was in a Sunday school classroom behind the microphone; Audrey, in another with the turntables and tape recorder. We were connected by a tangle of wires strung down the hall. It was a miracle how we ever made any programs worth airing, but we did! Mr. Welch, stumbling over a wire as he walked into one of the rooms, remarked, "What you need is a mobile studio."

His dear wife added, "And we will buy you one."

Seeing our tears and hearing how we had been praying for one, they said, "Go ahead. Pick out what you want, have it equipped, and send us the bill."

What an answer to prayer. We knew the Lord wanted us to broadcast!

We went from that meeting to the First Baptist Church of San Jose, California, for a revival. The Lord blessed mightily. The church took on new life. It was a revival. Just before the last service, the great pastor, Dr. Clarence Sands, said, "On Sunday night my men usually count the love offering right after it is taken, during the sermon. But they want to hear you preach. Do you mind if we count it Monday morning and send it to you?"

"No," I said, "we don't mind."

After the pastor and his wife joined us for breakfast the next morning, we left for Hollywood. On the way I asked, "Dear, do you know how much money I have right now?"

"No, but I'd like to."

"I'm broke," I confessed. "I gave my last dollar to the bell-hop." Then I asked, "How much money do you have?"

"I'm broke too," she answered. "I gave my last dollar to the maid."

I suggested that while we drove, she close her eyes and ask the Lord for ten dollars for food while I kept mine on the road.

Closing her eyes, Audrey prayed, "Dear Lord, the Bible says, 'The Lord is my shepherd, I shall not want.' We are in want. We need ten dollars. Please give it to us."

Just then a truck doing about seventy miles an hour passed us, shaking our car.

"What's that?" Audrey asked.

"Nothing," I told her. "Just a truck that passed us. Keep on praying; we need the money."

Suddenly the same truck ahead screeched to a stop, and the driver jumped out and came running right down the middle of the freeway toward our car. I pulled over, and as the driver came alongside Audrey asked, "What should I do?"

I told her to roll down the window just as the man pushed his head into the car and said, "I don't know you, and you don't know me. I've never seen you before, and I may never see you again. But as I passed your car, something said 'Give them ten dollars.'" He threw the money in Audrey's lap, ran back to his truck, and drove away. We sat there, crying and thanking the Lord that His Word is true; when He is our shepherd, we shall not want!

When we went to the First Baptist Church of Downey, California, we were praying that God would send us the best engineer in the profession to help us build our mobile studio and to design our permanent broadcast studio. On the first night about fifty men came forward. One said to us, "My name is Johnny Johnson. I work at ABC-TV, and I am one of the best engineers in the profession. When I came forward tonight to give my life to the Lord, He told me you have something for me to do. I want to do it. What is it?"

"Two things," we told him. "A wonderful couple has offered

to buy a mobile studio for us, and we need someone to sound-proof it and equip it for broadcasting. And when the Lord provides the land for a studio, we need someone to design the rooms for recording and taping."

"I'll do it," he said, "providing you won't offer to pay me."

That was no problem. How we cried for joy. Johnny Johnson and his wife took us to the Silver Streak Trailer Company, and we bought a beautiful trailer. The Johnsons parked it in their yard, soundproofed it, built the console, wired it, and equipped it. We rejoiced in God's goodness and the graciousness of the Welches and the Johnsons. Then Johnny said, "When the Lord gives you the lot for the studio, we'll come wherever it is, spend three months, design it, equip it, teach you how to engineer the broadcasts, and come back three months every year to tune up your equipment—if you promise not to pay us."

You can't beat the Lord, can you? He always does exceedingly abundantly above all that we ask or think.

We traveled for several years with our mobile studio, making many trips from Savannah to San Diego, from the Great Lakes to the Gulf of Mexico to conduct our crusades and tape our broadcasts. After unloading the magic props, we would park the mobile studio beside the church. Then, during the night, when it was the quietest, we would tape our fifteen-minute broadcast, *The Sower*. We set up a little office in Metter where Audrey's mother took care of our mail.

The Lord enabled us to make quality programs, but when we conducted crusades in large cities, the studio couldn't screen out all the noise. Many times we had to make and remake the programs—the sound of falling pecans when we taped outside or a flushing toilet when we taped inside was not uncommon, and we would have to start all over again. We prayed in earnest, "Oh, Lord, please give us a lot and a studio. Thou hast promised, 'My God shall supply all your needs.' Thank You, Lord, for Thy faithful kindness."

While we were conducting a subsequent meeting in Tulare, a charming Christian couple, Mr. and Mrs. Wayne Denning, asked us to settle there, assuring us that other Christians would join us. They promised to give us a lot and to build a house and studio for us. We promised to pray about it and give them an answer the following morning.

Very early the next morning a call came from the mayor of Metter, Harold Trapnell. He said, "We want you and Audrey to come to Metter—where everything's better—and build your studio. As a gift, we'll give you your choice of lots."

"Billions of thanks," I replied. "We will pray about it, and we'll let you know."

Audrey and I immediately called upon the Lord for His guidance. The Lord seemed to say, regarding Metter, "This is the way. Walk ye in it." When I gave Wayne Denning our answer, he was disappointed, but encouraged us to do nothing more or nothing less than God's will. The Dennings are dear to our hearts, and Wayne is now one of our board members.

When we returned to Metter, Mayor Trapnell drove us around town saying, "Take your pick of lots." We finally came to a beautiful area about two miles from the heart of town, on State 121, the Woodpecker Trail, at 600 North Lewis Street, and the Lord seemed to say, "This is the site." Harold was thrilled—it was his choice too.

"How much money do you have?" he asked.

"One hundred dollars," I replied, "but the Lord will give us all we need."

Shortly after that Mrs. Stanley Welch called and said that her husband had told her before his death that he wanted me to conduct his funeral service. "Will you and Audrey come?" she asked.

"Yes, ma'am," I said. "We'll leave immediately."

We hurriedly packed and boarded a plane for Colorado Springs, where we laid to rest the body of our beloved benefactor and friend. After the service, we were at the airport, preparing to leave when Mrs. Welch asked what we were praying for now.

"A studio," I answered.

"Before Stanley died," she told us, "he said he wanted to be generous to the Guidos. Here's sixteen thousand dollars."

How Audrey and I cried, and through our tears we thanked the Lord for the woman at our side, Mrs. Welch, and we praised the Lord for His boundless goodness.

Our Lord told us that there is rejoicing in heaven over a sinner who repents. I believe that when souls are saved through this ministry, the Lord calls the Welches to His side to celebrate with Him, saying, "Another soul repented because of your gift of the studio to the Guidos."

Mayor Trapnell wanted to know if any more money for the studio had come in and I told him of the sixteen thousand dollars. He said, "My brother, Bill, is a famous interior designer who studied in Italy as well as here in the States. He has been doing the interior designing for many of the finest offices in Atlanta. I know he will donate his services. His brother-in-law is an architect, and I'm sure he will be kind to you. Let's get started right away."

With this group and Johnny Johnson, the ABC engineer, we came up with the plans for our studio and went out for bids. The lowest came in at sixteen thousand dollars—exactly what we had! Isn't that just like Jesus?

The two professional men wasted no time in implementing the planning phase. *The Metter Advertiser,* aware that the experts were in town, asked the visiting architect, Kenneth Johnson, a member of the American Institute of Architects and the National Society of Professional Engineers, to contribute an editorial to the newspaper. He responded:

> How does an architect design a building for the Lord's work? I recently was commissioned to design the Welch Memorial Studio of The Sower for the work of Michael and Audrey Guido. This was not a church for His work but a unique studio for taping messages of the Lord delivered through Michael Guido.
>
> As I looked at the lot with its tall Georgia pines, my mind was asking this question: should the studio blend with the natural setting, or should it stand out in contrast? Both approaches are valid in design—which should it be?
>
> After spending several hours with the Guidos, the answer was apparent.
>
> The work of the Guidos and their helpers stands out

in a world of sameness, indifference and sin. The building should have the same qualities.

Standing out against the wonderful rough bark and long needles of Georgia pine, the studio will be a statement of simplicity, purity and beauty. White brick, sharp, clean, uncluttered lines with the accent on the red door (the blood of the Lamb) will remind the people of the work being done there for the Lord.

The interiors will furnish functional spaces and background for the most important feature—dedicated people at work for His cause. The maps and mailing material will be displayed as a design element rather than an aftersight, and the studio and control room will be more meaningful than just being technically correct. The study will be planned with a meditation garden adjacent, featuring a sculpture of "The Sower." This garden with the sculpture is not planned in the original budget, but I know a way will be made to include this symbol of inspiration to Michael and his work.

This is how an architect designs a building for important work. He meets the people involved. He feels the urgency and fervor along with the dedication. His prayer is that the design will aid in this work for our Lord.

A strong believer in symbolism, Michael had a hand in giving the design a spiritual significance.

BECAUSE ONE ENTERS heaven only by the blood of the Lamb, we painted our front door red. We want to preach Christ, and because He's pure, we used white bricks. In my study, one wall is papered with a beautiful design depicting the cross. Since it was an old rugged cross on which Christ died, one wall is made of rough pine boards.

Often when we ask the Lord for bread, He gives us peanut butter and jelly too. After the studio was completed, the builder, Tommy Tomlinson, returned a thousand dollars.

The mayor and other businessmen of Metter wanted us to have a home, so they gave us the lot adjacent to the studio. Audrey and I had fervently prayed for a house of our own, our very first house. Ken Johnson drew the plans, Bill Trapnell worked on the interior decorating, and in just a little while the Lord performed another wonder work and gave us the money, not only for the house, but also for the furniture. On our first night together there, we invited the Lord to make Himself at home in our brand-new house, lovely, but not lavish. We felt we had a little bit of heaven right here on earth with the house and the attractively furnished, wonderfully equipped studio in such a beautiful location.

Herman Talmadge, our United States senator from Georgia, brought the dedicatory address with the Statesmen Quartet furnishing the music. The city of Metter met the out-of-town visitors with open arms, inviting many of them to stay overnight in their homes. Audrey's cousin, a caterer, served her famous barbecue in Metter's recreation center. Hundreds came from all over the nation. The presence of the Lord was wonderfully felt. We will always remember with gladness and gratitude the day Mrs. Stanley Welch cut the ribbon on the Welch Memorial Studio.

Every broadcaster told us we could not make a go of broadcasting without asking for money and using canned music. They were greater than we were, wiser too; but we felt that the Lord wanted us to go this way and would enable us to do what He enjoined us to do. We found that His precepts carried His provisions and power. He was and is ever-present, all-sufficient, and never-failing.

Four enthusiastic supporters—C. B. Jones, a tax collector; Dr. Henry Sparks, a dentist; Dr. Allen Womble, an optometrist; and Dekle Banks, an insurance salesman—called on radio stations and persuaded the managers to air our fifteen-minute broadcasts five days a week without cost if we paid the postage both ways.

Those days of getting started were most exciting, but extremely difficult. I sold a 12-gauge shotgun, a handcrafted rod and reel, and everything I didn't need, to buy tapes. We cashed in my insurance policies and made every sacrifice possible, but it was worth it all. It was such an honor to exchange silver for souls. We could not have made it without Audrey's father and mother. Every day they brought us vegetables and fruit from their farm, and fish they caught. Being from the North, I wasn't used to grits, collard greens, blackeyed peas, fatback, and barbecued goat, but I found them delightfully delicious.

When an expensive piece of equipment was needed, a broadcaster visited. He said, "I have never heard you ask for money over the air, and I checked around town and found you don't ask anyone for money in person. Surely you have some wealthy friends you go to for help, don't you?"

"No, sir," I replied.

"Well," he wondered, "on whom do you depend?"

"The Lord."

"Just the Lord?"

"Yes. Just the Lord. But He's all that I need. Have the Lord, and you have all. He never forsakes in need the one who trusts in Him indeed."

One day Savannah's beloved broadcaster, Burl Womack, asked us to produce a ten-minute broadcast to augment a five-minute news segment his station aired. Lifting a quick prayer to the Lord, I felt He wanted us to do it. We call this *Your Favorite Ten*. It features one song and a five- or six-minute message. Don Wyrtzen orchestrated the opening and closing original theme.

Seeds from the Sower, a popular, five-minute broadcast, featuring an original theme by Ralph Carmichael, one song, and a ninety-second message, was produced in answer to broadcasters' requests for something that would better fit their schedule demands.

The one-minute spot, *A Seed from the Sower*, consisting of an original theme by Don Wyrtzen and my forty-two-second message, was developed to be slipped in before or after a newscast, or to be dropped in between breaks in a ball game—anywhere it could be used.

The Sower is fifteen minutes long. It begins with our sparkling theme, "Bringing in the Sheaves"; then we introduce two songs, and I bring a message about six minutes long.

One morning the phone rang at 5:30, and a man said, "I'm drunk. But I want you to know I like your program." Then he hung up.

The next morning he called again at 5:30. "Your program is beautiful. I like the way you talk, but I'm too drunk to talk with you today. 'Bye." I almost got the hiccups talking to him!

On the third morning he informed me, "I'm a bit sober. Man, you touched my heart. I need help. Pray for me."

The next morning I was waiting and praying for him at 5:30. This time he talked a little plainer: "I'm in a better mood," he said. "I can think better. Pray for me."

I did, sincerely, tenderly. "Thanks," he muttered. "I'll call tomorrow."

Right on time, he called the next morning and told me he was sober enough. "How can I be saved?" he asked.

"Ask Jesus to come into your heart," I told him.

"I ain't never prayed before," he cried. "Please help me."

"Follow me in this prayer," I instructed him. And I started, "Dear Jesus . . ."

He interrupted, "The only time I ever used His name was to damn somebody. Is it really all right for me to use it?" I assured him it was and he started again, "Dear Jesus . . ." He paused. "Ain't that name purty? Let me say it again." He whispered it over and over again and finally said, "I'm ready."

I led him in praying, "Dear Jesus, I open the door of my heart. I receive Thee. Please come in." Then I read Revelation 3:20: "Behold, I stand at the door and knock. If anyone hears My voice and opens the door, I will come in to him."

I asked, "What did Jesus do when you asked Him to come in?"

"He came in," he shouted.

"How do you know?"

"Because He said so, and He don't lie! He saved me! I gotta hang up and tell the old lady."

He called again the next morning and said, "I'm saved. It's okay. But my old lady sees such a big change in me, she wants to be saved too."

With the Lord Jesus giving us one station after another, we ran out of room in the studio. We needed more space, so Audrey and I prayed, resting on the promise that if we asked, it would be given us. "Please send us an architect, a very good architect, for our needed addition. Because we have asked, we know Thou wilt send us one. Thanks, Lord."

Our doorbell rang one evening shortly after and a stranger appeared at the door. "Hello. My name is Jim Buckley. I was flying my plane home to Swainsboro after a business trip when I heard your broadcast. I made a 180-degree turn, and here I am. If you need an architect, just yell." I let out a mock yell right on the spot, and Mr. Buckley asked, "What do you need?"

"Three rooms and storage space," I replied. I explained about his being an answer to our prayers. Mr. Buckley looked around the buildings and grounds to see where an addition might go.

"Okay, I'll do the designing, and it won't cost you anything," he told us. Then he listed his credentials just to set our minds at ease. A few days later he returned with plans for approval and asked when we could start construction.

"Just as soon as we get the money."

He asked, "Where will you get twenty-six thousand dollars? Do you have a wealthy board? Will you have a special fund-raising drive?"

"No, we're going to pray for it. Will you join us right now?" We all bowed our heads. "Dear Lord, thank You for Jim and his help. Your Word says, 'the Lord is my shepherd; I shall not want.' We are in want. We need twenty-six thousand dollars. Prove Your Word, Lord, and send it to us."

When we opened our eyes, Jim said, "I'd better get busy making the changes we agreed on."

From a distant city, a few days later, a letter came from a person we had never met. She wrote, "I am lonely, and I need help. So many things bother me. You have helped me with your four daily broadcasts. I believe you can solve my problems and help me. Please come, won't you?"

Of course we would come, and we arrived at the designated time, pulling up at the old, abandoned store that was her home. She had pans and buckets all around the rooms to catch the rain water that was dripping through the leaky roof. She told us about her problems and her questions, then said, "No one loves me. No one comes to help me. No one has time for a poor, old woman like me. Please help me."

For the next six hours we answered her questions. Then as we got up to leave she said, "You're loaded."

"No," I answered. "Why would you say that?"

"You never ask for money. Then you must have a rich board?"

When I told her we didn't, she continued, "Well, you must borrow from others and just fail to pay them back."

"No," I replied, "we have never borrowed anything."

"Then tell me," she persisted, "how do you get what you need?"

"We pray."

"What are you praying for now?"

"An addition," I said, knowing I was not hinting.

The very next day a registered letter containing a check for twenty-six thousand dollars arrived from her. You just can't beat the Lord!

Incidents such as this have inspired us to see how the Lord meets our needs. So many times the answers have come from unexpected sources, like this gift. Who would have thought she could have given this large contribution? Our Lord does work in mysterious ways His wonders to perform. "Faithful is He Who called you. . . . Whom He calls, He enables" (1 Thess. 5:24, KJV).

In God's faithfulness Johnson and his wife have returned to Metter for short periods to check on the equipment and help keep everything in good condition. One radio executive, impressed by the quality of the program tapes, asked Michael, "Who is your engineer? I'd like to hire him."

"My engineer is my wife, and you can't have her," he replied with the pride that is ever displayed for *his lady*.

The facilities of the Welch Memorial Studio produce the Sower's sermons that bounce by satellite and transmitter to unknown places, unnamed people, and fields of harvest.

Often Michael and Audrey are driven to work harder

and seek every possible way to better their work and increase their commitments. They are joyous reflections of God's promise that "he who sows and he who reaps may rejoice *together!*"

CHAPTER 5

We SHALL COME REJOICING

This is the day which the LORD has made;
We will rejoice and be glad in it.

Psalm 118:24

The contagious joy and rejoicing that accompany the Guidos are like flags displayed above their lives, over the gardens and the studio that heralds an unseen message: "Rejoice in the Lord always. Again, I will say rejoice" (Phil. 4:4).

Rejoicing is the centerpiece of their existence and the cornerstone of their ministry—rejoicing that another seed has germinated, another station was added, or a letter expressed gratitude for the ministry from a listener who had intended to write for twenty-eight years. Realities of change in the lives of their invisible audience are indeed their *raison d'etre!*

I'LL NO LONGER SERVE THE CLOCK, RATHER THE TIMELESS PLAN OF GOD

"I believe the Guidos' clock has added hours," confessed a Pennsylvania listener. "I'm told their lights are on around the clock. I've heard that they never really sleep." Although he may have overstated a bit, the gentleman who said this represents three generations of his family born again as a result of the ministry. He was once an alcoholic; his daughter, a cocaine user and a co-dependent; his ten-year-old granddaughter, in the habit of borrowing her mother's pills for a "high." It was the girl who first saw and listened to *The Sower*. Then she begged her mom and grandfather to watch for the "television gardener. He makes me feel better."

"The Sower is my salvation," the little girl said.

"No," corrected Grandpa, after months of watching, "Jesus is our salvation. The Sower was His messenger boy to us."

The third-grade girl exclaimed, "He sure brought the right message to this crazy, mixed-up family."

Board members, close friends, and associates would agree that the Sower and his lady keep an incredible schedule and must have acquired a clock with extended hours.

A curious reporter, determined to find the answer to such energy and diligence, spent a "typical" day with them to provide a minute-by-minute chronicle for his readers.

Michael Fluent, then news director of WMAC-AM/WHCG, Metter, and later editor of *Kindred Spirit*, a publication of Dallas Theological Seminary, recounted his stimulating but grueling day with the Guidos.

6:00—It is an ungodly hour to some, but to Michael Guido, early mornings are not only exhilarating but also a time for godly personal rededication.

6:30—He joins Audrey for a sunrise breakfast. The meal is light: one poached egg, one slice of unbuttered toast, a cup of coffee, and a small glass of orange juice.

7:00—Michael reads Scripture for their devotional time. Afterward, both pray.

7:15—Audrey retreats to the bedroom for her personal "quiet time" while Michael leaves for his office to enjoy his. He is dressed smartly in blue checked pants, white shirt, and light blue cardigan. Casual. Neat. In his study Michael explains, "I sometimes go through a book of the Bible. Other times a passage of Scripture like the Sermon on the Mount or the Lord's Prayer." Today it was the latter.

8:00—All too soon, quiet time is over, and the day's obligations begin. The staff are already in the conference room, one or two still bleary-eyed from the 7:00 waking. The very thought of Michael's reveille hour makes them shudder.

Michael shares a short message with them, usually no longer than a minute. . . . He spoke this morning on the words "Our Father." The rest of the group's quiet time is reserved for prayer. Each will pray, with Michael closing the session. Among today's petitions: a woman wrote that her sister is undergoing open-heart surgery; another said, "Pray for my divided home"; and a third asked that God guide her son in the choice of a career.

Michael and the staff also pray for the phone calls and letters of the previous day and night. "People see the telecast and they have questions. They want to know if they should do this or should do that. Is this all right, or should I do this? They have problems: marriage, family, school, work, and so on."

The group also pray for the items on the prayer board that the ministry sorely needs: a nine-thousand-dollar IBM electronic composer and a twenty-five-hundred-dollar stereo-mono cassette copier, to name just two.

8:15—Michael retires to his study to tackle the ever-increasing work load. The Sower Studios produce one-minute, five-minute, ten-minute, and fifteen-minute broadcasts as well as a one-minute telecast. In all, the Sower crew sends out thirty-five hundred radio, fifteen hundred television, and sixteen hundred newspaper messages every week!

First impressions indicate that Michael Guido has plenty of time to work since he'll be at his desk most of the day. First impressions, however, can be wrong, and second thoughts are in order.

Michael has interruptions. Plenty of them. At all times. "Last night at 11:00 an alcoholic called me. He'd seen our telecast and wondered if there was any hope for him. A college professor who didn't believe in God heard our broadcast and called. I led him to Jesus on the phone." A staggering number of calls come from blacks, and you needn't look far for the reason. There isn't one black pastor residing in Michael's home county, Candler.

12:00—Lunch time has Michael behind a sandwich, a bowl of soup, and a glass of iced tea.

12:20—Michael works on the grounds, picking up pine cones and cleaning out the man-made pools.

1:01—Even the boss is allowed only sixty minutes for lunch. There are several sermons yet to be written.

3:05—A Jewish man from Pennsylvania calls long distance, and Michael leads him to the Lord. The man had not been in any religious worship in fifteen years. Now, however, he is so transformed that he is going to have his wife call Michael this evening at 7:30.

6:00—The long afternoon winds down. The staff have left for their homes an hour ago. Michael goes to a dinner of spaghetti, salad, fruit, and coffee. "We only have dessert when we have guests," he jokes. If this were summer he would spend more time on the grounds and work there until dark. Because of the season, however, he retires to the living room. His favorite chair catches him, and his evening begins.

For the next several hours he will read a combination of books and magazines. The television is on, too, and his mind keeps account of both the book and the screen without any trouble. Usually the television holds little interest for him, but every so often a program captures his undivided attention.

7:30—The expected phone call comes. The Jewish man's wife is on the phone. Michael retreats into privacy.

7:50—Michael reappears, and his smile answers all

questions. A Jewish man and his wife are now believers.

11:30—The news is over. The book is put down. The magazine is laid aside. Faithfully, Michael Guido heads for his exercise bicycle. For the next thirty minutes he pedals vigorously at top speed.

12:00—The bicycle complains as Michael gets off. It is a matter of debate as to whether Michael or the bicycle got the most vigorous workout.

Nineteen-hour days—and longer—are typical for Michael—work takes precedence over sleep. "I can go to sleep now and get a call at any hour of the night. People have problems or prayer requests, and they want to know about salvation."

Audrey adds that today was not usual in one respect. "It is not uncommon for him to have a three- or four-hour counseling session during his day. I've seen Michael emerge from those sessions literally exhausted. By far, counseling is the hardest thing to do. In fact, Michael has many times counseled people for an entire day. And there have been numerous times when people have stayed with us for entire weekends while we just talked."

For sessions like these Michael needs an inexhaustible source of strength. And he has One. But he also practices a method to help himself. Audrey explains:

MICHAEL HAS A peculiar habit. If dinner isn't ready, he sits down in his chair and, in seconds, he is sound asleep. A five-minute nap for him is like an hour for anyone else.

Since Michael has had three heart attacks, he needs his rest. When he had his first attack, he was just thirty-one. His problem was that he couldn't relax. Now he does what his doctor says. He's trained his mind to relax and just wills himself to sleep. So he gets his five-minute naps. That way he can work until one in the morning and be ready to start the new day at six. Sometimes he can even continue straight through the night into the new day. And he can do it with grace.

When Michael finally comes to bed he says, "Good night, Audrey. I love you more now than I did this morning. Good night, Jesus. I'll see You in the morning." Even when we travel, we keep this schedule, with only a few small changes.

Part of the inspiration for keeping this grueling schedule is God's continuing care for the ministry's needs. Michael has stories to tell about God's provision:

LATE ONE AFTERNOON a lad walked in and asked "to see the Sower." I invited him into my office, and he said, "You led me to Jesus, Mr. Guido, and I'm here to thank you. I ain't got much— only a nickel—but maybe you can use it."

Shaking his hand and accepting his gift, I replied, "We sure can use it. It will buy one of our little gospel booklets, and the Lord can use it to save a soul."

The boy's eyes widened in his excitement: "Wow! A soul for silver."

That boy's gift is just one of many that keep our organization operating from day to day. We couldn't get along without them, and we rejoice in each one.

Here and there God blesses our ministry with a bonus gift, a large amount that will let us expand more quickly. Often some-one calls to ask what items are on our prayer board that day, but sometimes the blessing comes personally, right on the spot.

One morning Audrey and I were praying at the office, asking God for the funds to buy an offset duplicator that we needed badly in the print room. As we prayed we heard the door open, but we continued with our prayer. When we finished we opened our eyes and stood up to greet two men—strangers to us. They introduced themselves as Truitt Lively and his friend Cliff Williams from Texas.

They asked us if we had time to give them a tour of the studio, so we escorted them around the offices and gardens. They thanked us kindly and went on their way.

We continued praying for the duplicator in the months that followed. Then, a year later, a phone call came from Mr. Lively. "Did you ever get that offset duplicator you were praying for a year ago?"

"No, but we're still praying, and it will come in the Lord's good time."

"Do you know why it didn't come?"

"No, I don't. I've been asking the Lord if there's something wrong with me that hinders my prayers."

"It's not you. I'm the guilty party. The Lord told me to give you the money for it a year ago, and He's been talking about it ever since. Go ahead and buy the machine; Cliff and I will send you the money for it right away."

Later, when our ministry needed fifty thousand dollars for a studio addition, Mr. Lively and his wife, Barbara, borrowed that amount, using a 1.6-acre tract of land they had purchased as their dream home site as collateral, and gave it to the Sower for construction. In time, Mr. Lively sold the property to pay off the loan and realized a profit of almost fifty thousand dollars.

God teaches us lessons in obedience frequently. I believe our work continues to go forward because we learn that "to obey is better than sacrifice." Gently and not so gently, God nudges His people and activates the giving response.

Sometimes, too, God moves people to respond after many years. Audrey and I met Bob McSherry, an operations manager and real estate director for the R. S. Noonan Group, a building management firm in York, Pennsylvania. His son and daughter gave themselves to the Lord during one of our campaigns in York. Years later, he called, convinced that the Lord wanted him to find out what was presently on our prayer board.

Lila Williams answered the phone, and she responded to his request. She began with a greenhouse and was interrupted. "Hold it right there!" Bob said. "Let me speak to Michael, please."

We greeted each other warmly, and Bob asked, "May I have my man design you a greenhouse?"

"Is he a good architect?"

How Bob laughed before he said, "He designed a medical college and a big-city airport, among other things."

"Oh, he *is* good."

Bob said, "All right, then. I'll have him design it, and we'll come down and build it."

Not many days later three men from Pennsylvania pulled up in our driveway around 4:00 in the morning. They had driven all night from York to say, "We've come to build your greenhouse."

With help from a local contractor, Bobby Rigdon, these three men—Bob McSherry, Bob Parks, and Bob Mader (three Bobs and a Bobby, they called themselves)—put up a greenhouse in three days and three nights. Then they drove all night to make it back to their jobs by morning. And once again, the Lord used a long-term relationship to His glory.

On another occasion Bob called our offices to see if anything was needed for the new addition to the studios. "Yes," I said, a lot of things. Chairs, tables—"

"Virginia and I will buy them for you," Bob interrupted. And they did.

Our new addition brought on other needs as well. God met one of those needs when Herb Simmons, a master craftsman and one of our board members, saw that the desk in my office wasn't suitable. He asked if he might make me one. He did, and it's a beautiful and serviceable gift to the Lord's work.

> In that same simple way, friends often rally to the needs of the organization. Engineers offered their services when electrical problems faced the studio. They continue to call from time to time to see if there is another need. Such generous donations of time, energy, and talent have pushed the Sower's timetable ahead significantly. Some friends have continued to wonder about the fund-raising philosophy. Michael always gives the same answer:

WHEN GERALD ACHENBACH, a retired Piggly-Wiggly executive and a golfing legend, asked me why I don't ever ask for money, I told him, "We promised the Lord that we would trust Him for all our needs. He hasn't let us down yet."

Everything on the grounds—the studio, equipment, furnishings, houses, plants, and accessories—has come in answer to prayer. Our friends and supporters have shown their loyalty to the Lord and to His work. For example, when we saw that we urgently needed a print room addition, we began our campaign of intercession. As we prayed, Tom Whichard called us from Florida. I said, "Hello, Tom, I remember you well. When we were in Florida about fifteen years ago for meetings in your church, you were our gracious host for lunch one day."

"Yes, that's right," he said. "You have been a blessing to me, and I'd like to do something for you. I read about your need for a new print room in *Sowing and Reaping*. What do you need?"

"About sixty-five thousand dollars."

He sent it to us, and today the Dorothy and Thomas Whichard Print Room is a vital part of our ministry. Since then, they've also purchased a much-needed typesetting machine and a word processor for the work.

Another time, when the offset duplicator needed updating, we all prayed for a later and better model. Gerry Achenbach, who brought some friends from Augusta to tour the studio one day, introduced them to me and said, "I have a gift for you. I'll see you before we leave." When the tour was over, he and his friends left without another word.

Several days later Gerry returned. "I saw that you needed a new offset duplicator, and I went home and wrote out a bigger check. Here it is."

Another time Gerry brought a young man in to see me for spiritual counsel. God's wisdom and Word worked together to help the young man solve his problem. Then I took both of them on a tour of the offices. When he came to the prayer board, Gerry said, "I see you need a word processor. You should pray for a Lanier."

"I will," I said.

Within a few days, Gerry came back and said, "The Lord laid it on my heart to buy the Lanier for you. Here's the money."

Yet another time La and Hal Woodward called from San Jose: "It's been a long time since you preached in our church," they said. "We've missed you. May we come see you?" They came, toured the studio, enjoyed the gardens, and left after a couple of days.

"We wondered why the Lord laid it on our hearts to come," they phoned after returning home. "Now we know. While looking at your prayer board, we saw that you are praying for a lot to build a warehouse on. We want to buy that lot for you."

One evening Joe Hamstra, a board member, and his wife, Bonnie, called and asked, "What do you want more than anything else in the world?"

"A warehouse," I said instantly.

"More than anything else?"

"Yes. We need a place to store paper and other material. Right now, it's scattered all over town."

"What size do you need?"

"About 60' by 100'."

"It's yours."

You can't beat the Lord, can you?

REJOICE! REJOICE! REJOICE!

God continued to use people who were sensitive to His voice to help meet a need of the Sower ministry. Like many other gifts, a pickup truck was donated in a roundabout way. Mike Warren, manager of the Coca-Cola plant in Statesboro, furnished free Cokes for the dedication of the new Whichard Print Room. He learned that the staff was praying for a pickup truck to haul packages to the post office and to carry equipment for repair. Michael tells what happened.

A FEW DAYS later Mike Warren sent one of his men to the Sower offices, towing a pickup truck. "Do you want it?" the driver asked.

"We certainly do. Thank you very much."

"Well," the driver said, "the motor is in good condition, but you'll need a transmission and a clutch."

"No problem," I replied.

"Before you can start it, you'll need a battery."

"No problem."

"You will probably want to paint it and buy a new fender."

"No problem. We can do these things. I just want to thank you and Mike Warren again for making this possible."

Over the next few days we bought a clutch and a transmission from a junkyard. We got the truck running, but the transmission was giving us trouble. So I called my friend, Curtis Lewis, a former mayor of Savannah, who owned three television stations and a Ford dealership: "Curtis, what can you allow us for our pickup? I'd like to trade it for a later model." I described the truck, with all its defects.

Lewis laughed and said, "If you promise not to bring it to my lot, I'll give you a new Ford pickup as a gift."

A few days later the Sower had a brand-new truck for the ministry, and we sold the worn-out pickup for seven hundred dollars. What better evidence do we need that "faith is the substance of things hoped for, the evidence of things not seen" (Heb. 11:1).

Audrey had a chance to answer another question often asked by outsiders: How does the Lord continue to supply needs? A newscaster interviewed her on the subject one day:

HE WAS IMPRESSED with the sophistication of our equipment and the scope of our ministry, but he wanted to know where we get the enormous amount of money we need to carry on. I was pleased to tell him that it comes from a variety of sources—not just radio and television contacts but also evangelistic services, church budgets, and even some Sunday school classes. Our primary source of funds is individuals giving an average of five dollars. We do receive some large donations, but they're usually one-time gifts from people who are burdened for a specific cause. That is the way we like it, and you can see that we naturally pray for more burdened souls.

Of course, the interviewer wanted to know then if we had ever asked for money. I told him, "No. Long ago we promised the Lord that we would never make a direct appeal for money. And we have never broken that promise." Michael and I thank the Lord daily that we have never had to break it.

The interviewer continued, "Can people designate their money for a certain purpose?"

I said, "Oh, yes. Many of our donors designate: One man wants his money to go to the printed word, another to radio, a third to the telecasts. When no specific request is indicated, the money is used for operational expenses. We record the names of loved ones in whose name a donation is made in a Book of Remembrances. But if someone asks, a gift goes toward one of the various pieces of equipment we need. That's how we acquired the stereo equipment. Someone else gave the money for the lending library.

In response to his question about where a donor's money goes, I gave him a broad financial breakdown: "Mostly to the ministry, but also for administrative expenses and salaries. The telecasts cost forty-five thousand dollars a year—that tremendous expense alone is inconceivable to most people. Printing runs about five thousand dollars a month; our electric bill is fifteen hundred; recording supplies, another thousand. Our smallest expense is vehicle upkeep. Even with all the traveling we do in a year, it only costs us two thousand for the cars and the truck. In contrast, postage is three thousand a month. We have an annual budget of $365,000, our total assets are more than a million dollars, and we're debt free."

That last bit of information surprised him so much that he asked for more details. I told him, "We don't make purchases until we have the capital. We never burden ourselves with mortgages when we build. Personally, I couldn't work or live under the pressure of debt, so we wait on the Lord until the money is available."

Since I can remember when our annual budget was only six thousand dollars, I had to agree with the interviewer when he commented on the accelerating amount of our expenses. He wondered next if inflation had hurt us, and I told him, "To some extent, but we've always met our bills. It may have reduced some people's giving, but we are getting more money than ever before to meet our greater expenses. Our outreach has increased, so naturally expenses soar. Costs for tapes, paper products, and packaging have doubled in recent years, and postage has gone up to twenty-five cents for a first-class letter."

Like many of our visitors, the interviewer wondered about our new memorial garden. He asked if it was an outgrowth of our practice of letting people donate money for a specific purpose. I told him, "Yes. We place a plant in the garden in the memory of a loved one who has passed away. The donation goes into the ministry, and a marker with the names of the deceased and the donor is placed by the plant. We like to think that the Lord will say to that loved one in heaven, 'Rejoice with Me! A gift given in your memory just brought a soul to repentance.'"

He looked admiringly at the garden and said, "For just that serene setting, I think your ministry is worth the sacrifice."

"Well," I told him, "it's been rough at times, but I have no regrets. As I look back over our lives and ministry, I don't think I would have changed anything or done anything differently."

Their personal generosity may account somewhat for the liberality of so many others. That same characteristic may in part open up the numerous opportunities Michael and Audrey find to be the salt and light in their own private world, a world handled with prayer and generous rejoicing—bringing in the sheaves.

CHAPTER 6

Bringing in the Sheaves

He who goes to and fro weeping, carrying his bag of seed, shall indeed come again with a shout of joy, bringing his sheaves with him.

Psalm 126:6, NAS

ONE DAY TWO successful businessmen in their early thirties came to see me. They had been listening to our daily broadcasts and telecast and the Lord had prepared their hearts.

Ready to receive the Lord, we dropped to our knees to pray. One called on the Lord saying, "Here we are, Lord, two s.o.b.'s, and we want to be saved. I now receive Thee." The Lord, according to His Word, made him His son.

The other prayed, "Lord, I open the door of my heart. Please come in right now." The Lord Jesus came in. Immediately arising, the man went to everyone in our studio and confessed the Lord.

This young man, Gary, called the next day from Savannah, telling me that one of the waitresses in his restaurant had noticed the change in him. "May I bring her to your studio?" he said. "She would like to talk to you also."

They arrived about two hours later, and she said, "When Gary got back to the restaurant, he told everyone he had received the Lord as his Savior. All of us were surprised at his turn-around experience. I want what he has." She too received the Lord.

About a month later, he called again and asked, "What must I experience to lead a soul to the Lord?"

"Salvation," I told him.

"You mean that's all?" His surprise was evident. "I don't have to be licensed or ordained or anything? Then let me hang up right now and lead this one to the Lord. Good-bye." I discovered later that he did, indeed, lead a good friend to Christ.

About a year later, after three surgeries for brain cancer, Gary was told that no medication, treatment, or other surgery could help him. My volunteer pilot, Ellis Wood, flew me to see Gary in Mobile, Alabama. He had failed so fast, but was still able to recognize me. I asked him, "What's the good word, Gary?"

"Jesus loves me," he quickly answered.

While he slept, his mother showed me the Bible I had given him. On closer inspection I noticed that many verses were underlined and checked—verses on two subjects: forgiveness and heaven.

Many of the underlined verses he had committed to memory:

If we confess our sins, He is faithful and just to forgive us our sins and to cleanse us from all unrighteousness.
1 John 1:9

Let not your heart be troubled; you believe in God, believe also in Me. In My Father's house are many mansions; if it were not so, I would have told you. I go to prepare a place for you. And if I go and prepare a place for you, I will come again and receive you to Myself; that where I am, there you may be also.   John 14:1–3

I left Gary rejoicing in his heavenly Father and his heavenly home last week, thanking the Lord he was safe in the arms of Jesus.

When it rains, it pours. Troubles come in teams. We had been using two stitchers to staple our devotionals and sermons, and both broke simultaneously. One was too old to repair; the other, too ornery. We could not find parts for one; the factory-trained technicians gave up on the other. We gave ourselves to prayer.

Audrey, Lila, and Sue, with our printer and his wife, visited a print show and checked out the stitchers, looking to the Lord for guidance in choosing the right one for our ministry. Finding a four-head Rosback Auto-stitcher, they tried it out, convinced that this was the one. The only thing wrong was the cost: twelve thousand dollars.

The owner of a nursery in Dearing, Georgia, Mr. C. S. Mc-Corkle, visited the gardens, which were in full bloom. Thrilled to see the hundreds of plants he and his sons had donated, he learned that we had been praying unceasingly for this new piece of equipment. Sweetly and humbly he asked if he might make the purchase for us.

Along with the McCorkles, we had a heart warming dedication service for the new stitcher, giving it and ourselves to the Lord and thanking Him for His goodness.

Sometimes a good laugh is just what we need. In one of our meetings the pastor was going through a time of trial, and we joined him in prayer. While we were praying his little son slipped in, and listened attentively. When we got up from our knees, he asked, "Dad, what's wrong with Mom? Don't you love her anymore?"

The pastor was puzzled, "Of course I love your mother. What do you mean?"

"Well," he explained, "I heard you pray for God to give you grace. Grace is my Sunday school teacher's name. I thought you loved her instead."

And sometimes service brings us great joy. A thrilling honor came my way one day. I was invited to offer the opening prayer for the United States House of Representatives. With much prayer, I asked the Lord to make me worthy of the privilege and a blessing to the members of Congress.

The chaplain thought the prayer was very appropriate:

> Heavenly Father, we thank Thee that Thou art always present, all-sufficient, and never-failing. Accept our gratitude for our president, our speaker, and the members of Congress. Grant them Thy wisdom for their minds, Thy strength for their bodies, Thy love for their hearts, and Thy grace for their souls. Be pleased, Father, to control and take charge of our deliberations and deci-

sions, bringing them into harmony and homage to Thy Holy will. Grant Thy blessings upon our companions and children, our country and citizens. Make us adequate for every advantage, equal to every emergency, and triumphant in every task. In Thy name, Amen.

Afterward, several people handed me cards, asking me to pray for them by name. Some even wrote specific requests on the cards. Audrey and I faithfully prayed for these.

At lunch with some of the Congress members, I was bombarded with questions about the Lord and His Word. It was one of the most refreshing luncheons I have ever enjoyed, and how comforting it was to know that we have so many Christians in the House of Representatives.

While resting in my hotel room before boarding the plane to return home, I received a call from a congressman's administrative aide, asking me to talk to a man who had been refused a political appointment and was now threatening to do something drastic. After our conversation, the man turned his life over to the Lord, saying that he needed salvation much more than a political appointment.

The experiences of serving as chaplain of the day for the Senate and House of Representatives in Atlanta have been equally rewarding.

Just recently as I was driving home after addressing a civic club, I saw the flashing lights of a highway patrol car in my rearview mirror. By the time I stopped and got out of the car, the trooper was at my side. Throwing his arms around me, he apologized for giving me a fright. "I just wanted to meet you. I gave my life to the Lord watching your telecast, and I wanted to thank you."

Returning from a speaking engagement, rejoicing in the blessings of the Lord, I heard the siren and saw those flashing lights again. "Hello, Mr. Guido," the trooper said. "We need you. You bless our hearts with your broadcasts. We want you around for a long time. *Please slow down!* God bless you." Wow! What a sweet way to correct an errant preacher. Needless to say, I stayed within the speed limit all the way home.

About one thousand people tour the studio and gardens every month. Just before leaving, three black women came through my study. It was a joy to pray for them. Then one of the saints prayed a prayer of her own: "Lord, what a memory we will have of visiting the Sower. Help us to keep it fresh in the refrigerator of our hearts, to bake it in the ovens of our minds, and to store it in the temple of our lives. Glory!"

What a prayer! She did my heart good.

While conducting a revival in St. Louis, on my morning walk, I saw a fellow staring down into the water below the bridge where he was standing. "Thinking of jumping?" I asked. When he said that was what he intended and his problems were just too big, he wondered what I would do.

"I am sure your problems are big," I told him, "but God is bigger. Come with me to my motel room, and let's talk about it." He came. We talked. We read the Bible. We prayed. I suggested that he turn over all his problems to the Lord. He rolled off all his grief, and the Lord rolled in His grace. Henry turned his life over to the Lord, happily and wholly. Peace filled his soul, and he went out to live a victorious life.

During an area-wide revival in Illinois, about a month later, Audrey and I were having dinner at the home of a gentleman. As we sat down at the table, I noticed an envelope on my plate. Since there was no name on it, I put it to one side. Our host insisted that I open it. Inside there was a generous gift with a note expressing a father's thanks for the help we had been to his son, Henry. The money was to be used for a trip to the Holy Land during the next twelve months—while we were still young in the ministry, our host stipulated. When we help others, the Lord sees to it that others help us.

That was how I came to make my first trip to the Holy Land. It was an inspirational blessing. The Lord allowed me to make other trips, teaching the Bible all through that land and Europe. This helped me in my ministry and opened up exciting doors. That tiny place, full of history, is central and meaningful to believers.

One of the doors it opened was to a synagogue. One of Augusta's outstanding dentists was working in my mouth. "You're my favorite TV star," he said. "I watch you every morning, and I enjoy the telecasts. Would you come to my synagogue and give a talk?" He called to tell his rabbi that the Sower would be honored to speak at their synagogue. The rabbi expressed his pleasure and asked what my topic would be so they could advertise it.

Looking to the Lord in a short prayer, I told him "Israel, the Land I Love."

On the given Saturday, I arrived early and attended the regular prayer meeting. I followed along in English while they said their prayers in Hebrew. My heart was blessed. Afterward, we gathered for a delicious breakfast, and I brought the message the Lord had laid on my heart: I love Israel because of the promise, the productivity, the patriotism, and the presents—she gave me the Scriptures and the Savior. The message was well received. The gracious rabbi commented on my enjoyment of following the Hebrew psalms and prayers and presented me with a book in English and Hebrew. "You do know a little Hebrew, don't you?"

"Yes, sir," I assured him. "My dentist."

It has been a pleasure to give talks at various clubs, such as the Italian Club of Savannah. After a warm and royal welcome, the president told me how much he enjoyed our programs. "I want you to know I'm trying to be a Christian," he said.

"Why don't you try to be an elephant?" I asked. "You can no more become a Christian by trying than you can become an elephant through effort. You become a Christian by trusting the Savior."

That banquet was held on Columbus Day, and I spoke on Columbus. I reveled in his love for our Lord and His word. The meeting was mightily blessed, and some of the club officers later came to our studio and received the Lord Jesus.

The chairman and pastor of the First Baptist Church in Elmhurst, Illinois, and his wife, the Reverend and Mrs. Jack MacDonald, felt led to go as missionaries to Venezuela under the Evangelical Alliance Mission. They asked us to come and hold meetings in the interior. We accepted the challenge with joy. I asked the missionaries and ministers, "What is your greatest hindrance to the cause of Christ?"

They did not list cults or witchcraft or false religions; they said, "Hypocrites."

When we had meetings in the interior, whole villages came to Christ. However, in areas where they had had contact with hypocrites, it was awfully hard to lead the lost to the Lord. How vividly this brought home to my heart that the greatest hindrances to the cause of Christ are un-Christlike Christians. I found myself asking the question, "Am I so unlike Christ that it would help His cause if no one ever saw me again?"

A choice interpreter, Jack took us to village after village to give out the gospel. We left an area where many had been saved to go on to the next. That night a man came, asking us to come see a national Christian who was dying of cancer.

Jack drove us to a small hut where we met the woman. She rejoiced in the conversions of the night before, telling us through Jack that until then she had been the only Christian in that big area. She had been praying that the Lord would let her live, even in the pain of her cancer, until someone got saved. What a heartwarming time we had praising the Lord. She told us that when the pain got so intense that she couldn't walk, she got down on her hands and knees and crawled to the village to pray and witness to the people. "Now they're saved," she said, "the Lord has Christians there, and I'm ready to go to heaven. Please pray with me that our Lord will take me home to heaven right away."

Afterward, she asked us to sing with her, "When the Roll Is Called Up Yonder." Never have we heard it sung so sweetly. As I walked away, I asked myself if I would have walked in pain to witness to the lost; if I would have crawled on my hands and knees to save souls in spite of the physical hardship. The Lord laid a burden on my heart through that Christian in a remote village in Venezuela.

Some of our biggest blessings have come from meetings in the smallest communities. Before the last meeting in a series in Kansas, a deacon asked Audrey and me to have dinner with him. While we enjoyed the food, the deacon asked me if I had ever had measles. When I told him that I hadn't, he said, "Well, you're going to have them now. All of my kids sitting around the table have them. I wanted to see how you'd react."

I smiled, enjoyed the dinner and preached, and the Lord blessed with conversions.

A few days later we opened a meeting in Hennessey, Oklahoma, in another small country church. The pastor and the people had the biggest hearts we ever met anywhere. We stayed with the Reverend and Mrs. Wallace Linton, who drove us to the church over the unpaved country roads every night. We could not start the first night—it had been one rain storm after another. After a night or two we got to church on a "shove and prayer." I got out in the rain and mud and shoved! I loved it—I'd do anything for those precious people—but I got sick. Awfully sick.

Sure that the deacon's prediction had come to pass, Audrey insisted on taking me to see a doctor. I really didn't want to because I was afraid we would have to cancel the meetings. The diagnosis was confirmed—I had measles. After talking to Audrey, the doctor let me conduct the meeting if I entered and left by the rear door and avoided any contact with the members. Nobody else got sick, and we had a special revival. Sinners were saved, backsliders were restored, and Christians were consecrated. We have returned for many meetings with those dear folks we love.

Metter Radio, WMAC, aired our fifteen-minute broadcast, *The Sower*, every morning before school started. One morning about 8:30 a young man, reeking of alcohol and bleeding from the wrists, rushed through our door. "I want to be saved. Help me!"

While Audrey applied bandages, the young man said, "I'm a con artist. I've been drinking heavily, I can't hold a job, and my marriage is falling apart. I was sitting in a liquor store, drinking, trying to end it all. Then I heard your broadcast. You gave me hope. I want to be saved. Help me."

I read the Word of the Lord, and explained simply and shortly how to be saved, and we fell to our knees. After I had prayed, the young man followed, asking the Lord to come into his heart and save him. It seemed as if a nail-pierced hand came down from heaven and washed his sins from him. He became a brand-new person. He ran from the studio, promising to be back in a jiffy. Sober now, he jumped into his car and soon came back with his wife and kids. She was thrilled with his transformation, and she wanted a life-changing experience too.

Our new friend's conversion brought him victory over alcohol and drugs. But he still had a terrible time holding a job and paying his debts. He owed everybody and their friend. Nobody would hire him. After we found him a job, Audrey suggested that he bring his paycheck to her and she would give him money for living expenses and manage his finances. He agreed. We saw to it that he, his wife, and his children were nicely clothed, properly fed, and happily cared for. He worked very hard and well. The plan was successful. Everyone began to look up to him and his wife. They left Metter with money in the bank, bought businesses in Savannah, and are living happily for the Lord.

Michael and Audrey Guido have shed their tears for lost souls. As the opening verse in this chapter reads, they have gone "to and fro covering vast parts of this world," and the "weeping for a night" has brought "joy in the morning." For they are "carrying his bag of seed." Scattered for the successful young businessmen, self-described s.o.b.'s but redefined, after Christ, as the Savior's Overjoyed Believers! Seed bearing another kind of fruit in the long-needed, high-quality stitcher for the print shop. Seed sprouted in the heart of a very desperate husband and father on the precipice of a bridge. Seed cast on good ground at civic clubs, synagogues, and the House of Representatives. "The seeds shall indeed come again," and with a "shout of joy." Michael and Audrey humbly thank the true and ultimate Sower for the privilege of "bringing His sheaves with them."

PART TWO

CHAPTER 7

SOWING
IN THE
SUNSHINE

It is good to give thanks to the LORD . . .
To declare Your lovingkindness in the morning,
And Your faithfulness every night. . . .
O LORD, how great are Your works!
Your thoughts are very deep.

Psalm 92:1, 2, 5

It was a bright, sunshiny day in Orange, Texas. All systems were go for Audrey Guido to drive a convertible, blindfolded, through the city streets. Accompanying her would be the pastor of a local church that would soon begin a revival. In the back seat would be a police officer. "I hope we make it," said the nervous pastor.

"Hope is hard to hold on to," remarked the officer. "This is a new experience for me. I thought I'd seen it all."

What prompted this feat by a daring young evangelist's wife? On arriving, Audrey and Michael had been informed by the pastor that a circus was coming to town on Friday night. He was very concerned about drawing any kind of crowd with that kind of competition.

Audrey volunteered for two things: "I'll drive a convertible blindfolded through the city," she told the pastor. "You and a police officer will ride with me. Next, you nail me in a box and I'll escape from it in thirty seconds."

The stunned pastor, Dr. Cooper Waters, was quick to accept the bizarre suggestion. "Let's go for it!"

They got official permission for the blindfolded drive. The stunt was organized, including getting the police officer to bring thirty feet of bandage with which to wrap her face. He covered her eyes completely—on top of rubber sponges placed over each eye. Then over the bandages came a black hood, which had been carefully examined by the spectators after the police officer tried it on and could not see through it.

Then she was led to the convertible.

Groping her way into position, she revved up the engine and started her blindfolded journey through the city streets. Passersby looked on in disbelief. People shouted, "That's incredible!" Audrey kept driving! The crowds grew larger and more enthusiastic.

Audrey was starring in her own show—a show to direct people to the church and to the Lord. It never failed to bring the crowd nor did God fail—many in that crowd were won to Him.

There were always those who felt that magic tricks could not glorify the Lord—they did not like it and felt it was wrong. Michael often countered with "Do you like to fish?" Usually a yes was the response. "What do you use for bait?" he continued.

"Worms," was the answer most given.

He quietly made his point: "Well now, I don't personally like worms—but the fish sure do."

Magic or illusion is sometimes classified as one effect— that of change or alteration in seemingly impossible ways. At this, Audrey became masterful—for her Master. It was also fun. She and Michael could perform as "partner acts," acts in which the two people involved are of equal importance and work as a team rather than performer and assistant. "Partner acts" have marked their lives as he sows and she maintains, as he crusades from the foreground and she conserves from the background.

To the church in Orange, Audrey had made two

suggestions to draw a crowd. One had been fulfilled in driving blindfolded. The next would be negotiated as always. Michael, again with obvious delight in "his lady," shares the preparation:

ON THE FIRST night of the one-week crusade, I asked if there were any carpenters in the audience. On identifying them, I asked if they would make a box to fit Audrey. They were to select the lumber. The box usually was built in a night and put on display in a bank or store with a sign stating that Audrey Guido, the Magic Lady, would be nailed in this box on Friday night at 8:00 at the civic auditorium and then make her escape.

On the given night, the box was brought to the meeting place and put up on the platform. Carpenters and undertakers were called at the appropriate time to nail down the lid.

Surrounded by those who were to do the hammering, Audrey asked for a man who was good at tying knots to come forward to tie her hands behind her back. The spectator could tie the knots in any fashion and as many times as he wanted. When he was satisfied, he turned to go back to his seat, and as he did, Audrey reached out, shook his hand, and thanked him for his participation. The poor fellow was flabbergasted.

Audrey said, in effect, "While sin thrills, it ties; while it fascinates, it fastens—but if the Son shall make you free, you shall be free indeed."

Then she asked the carpenters to kick the box on the sides and bottom to see if it was really sturdy. My, how they'd kick. The pan of nails was brought in. I held up a curtain briefly so that Audrey could get into the box comfortably, then dropped the curtain. The carpenters picked up the lid, put it on the box, checked to make sure Audrey and no one else was in it, then started nailing it shut. When they were sure that it was impenetrable, they left the platform. I said, "Dear, if you are still in the box, knock on the sides, or stick your fingers through the hole and wiggle them."

Again I lifted the curtain, showing only my hands on the curtain rod, and started slowly counting, "1, 2, 3, 4" and Audrey said "5," dropping the curtain in front of the box. She asked,

"Where's Mr. Guido?" and I began knocking. The carpenters came back up, pried off the lid—and there I was in the box, wearing a different sport coat!

Audrey pointed out that sins are like spikes: every time we sin, we drive another spike into our suffering, shutting ourselves up in our sorrow. But just as the Lord was raised from the tomb, so will He raise the one who believes in Him from his transgressions. And "if any man be in Christ, he is a new creation."

As our partner act continued, she asked me to stand at the other side of the platform, holding an empty crystal casket in my hands. Pointing a gun at me, she shot 1, 2, 3 times; and every time the audience heard a shot, a silk appeared in the crystal casket. Audrey used this to point out how our Lord makes all things work together for good. The shots don't blast or blight us; they only beautify us. Chastisement is not to destroy us, but to develop us.

Some nights before I preached, she asked me to stand in front of the congregation, and she spoke softly to me. Then she laid me on a table. The local pastor and his song leader then removed the frame of the table, leaving me suspended in midair while she passed a hoop over my body several times. How she thrilled the audience by saying, "underneath are the everlasting arms" of our loving Lord. Even though man can't see His arms, they are there, holding us safely and securely; no one, neither Satan nor sinner, can take us from His hands.

What prompted Audrey to turn to magic? After she heard the comments on her first visit to Moody that Michael should never have married a wife who had no musical talent or who could make no specific contribution to his ministry, she prayed for a unique and complementary service.

She kept searching the Word and seeking the Lord for ways to sow her seeds. One night at a Bible conference she saw Dr. Warren Filkin, a great and gifted magician, perform. "This is it!" she said. "I believe the Lord wants me to present Magic with a Message."

At Dr. Filkin's suggestion the Guidos visited Ireland's

Magic Shop in Chicago and bought a trick. It came so easily, she became fascinated. They purchased more equipment, and with Dr. Filkin's encouragement and help, Audrey became more skillful. The Lord mightily blessed her ministry.

During meetings in California, Audrey met originators of big stage tricks who took a liking to her and went the second mile to help. They built impressive stage effects for her that continued to be a source of new illusions. These were made by Merv Taylor and continue to hold fascination and conviction for many audiences. The Lord kept using the Magic with a Message to draw crowds to the crusade, then to Christ.

Audrey's college major made her familiar with chemicals. Looking to the Lord for inspiration, she used that knowledge to develop some exciting object lessons. The Guidos carried the chemicals in a custom-made container, which she and Michael could slip under their train seat. On a trip to Kansas the train stopped suddenly, and the jolted box released a terrible odor. Soon the porter, pinching his nose shut with his fingers, arrived and demanded to know where that old polecat was hiding. Michael pointed to the container, and the porter picked it up with the hand not holding his nose. With a quick toss, he pitched the entire box off the train. That was when Audrey sought new ways to serve the Lord through the ministry of Magic with a Message.

THE BUSH THAT BURNS, BUT IS NOT CONSUMED

Audrey presented the custom-built, ordinary-looking bush. It was about four feet high. Suddenly, the bush burst into flames, but would not burn up. It always startled the audience, and there was a hush as she presented her application: As Moses was carrying out his everyday occupation, in the common place of labor, the Lord revealed Himself to him. Even though it was a common place, it was a common place touched by the Lord God. But Moses had to "turn aside." Just as the Lord appeared to Moses where he lived and labored, so will the Lord appear to you, if you'll just turn aside as Moses did. Moses saw the flames. They represented the glory of the presence and power of the Lord, which transforms, but doesn't consume us. Like the bush, you and I may be unattractive and unprofitable, yet we can be transformed by the presence and power of the Lord and not be consumed. It was Cowper who wrote:

> Jesus, where'er Thy people meet,
> There we behold Thy mercy-seat;
> Where'er they seek Thee, Thou art found,
> And every place is hallowed ground.

THE ALTARS OF THE LORD AND THE PROPHETS OF BAAL

Audrey presented two Merv Taylor altars, each three feet square. On Baal's altar, she placed the meat and uttered the words of the prophets of Baal. There was no answer. She recounted how they called all morning but had no reply. They raved all afternoon—no response. Then Audrey turned to the altar of the Lord and placed the meat on it. She asked people from the audience to bring pitchers of water and taste it to verify that it was water; then she soaked the meat, and uttered Elijah's prayer, "Lord, answer me so these people will know that You are God!" Fire fell on the altar, licking up the water and consuming the meat. The stunned audience was told, "The effectual, fervent prayer of a righteous man availeth much." After a word about prayer, Audrey pointed out that God, in His wrath, could have consumed the people, but the fire only consumed the sacrifice. This reminds us that while we were yet sinners, Christ, our sacrifice, died for us.

THE BLOOMING ROSE BUSH

Audrey presented a Taylor-made bare rose bush, about
three feet high. While Audrey looked at it and spoke,
about a dozen roses appeared—first a little speck, then
getting bigger and bigger, finally dancing a graceful
minuet. Cutting the roses, handing them to people in
the audience, Audrey asked if their lives revealed Jesus,
the Rose of Sharon, and if their fragrance was like that of
the Rose of Sharon.

WE USED A custom-built trailer to carry our magic and traveled
all over the United States. In one city where we had a hard time
getting publicity, Audrey said, "Let's see what I can do." After
eating in a local restaurant and seeing some policemen in a booth
behind us, she asked, "Ready for some fun? Shall I make
money?"

"By all means," I replied as I handed over the check and
trailed to the cash register behind her.

She pretended to go through her bag, looking for money to
pay the bill, all the while ignoring the cashier and talking to me
as if we were the only people there. She said, "I guess I'll have to
make some money," as she asked the cashier for a blank piece of
paper. Audrey put the paper in a little gadget, turned the crank,
and pulled out a twenty-dollar bill, which she handed to the
cashier.

The girl cried, "Help! Police! There's a counterfeiter here."

The police were there in a moment, and so was a newspaper-
man with a camera. The angry cashier repeated what Audrey had
done. I glanced at a policeman, who winked at me and said, "Do
it again. Let me get real close to you. I want to catch you red-
handed." As he got close, watching Audrey and the trick, she
put another blank piece of paper in, cranked the handle, and
produced another twenty-dollar bill. By now, the flashbulbs
were popping, and a TV reporter held up his microphone. The
police officer said, "You're the Magic Lady my kid has been
talking about. The kids love you. The whole neighborhood's
wild about you. I'm coming to the meeting tonight."

Talk about publicity—we got it! After that we didn't lack for a crowd.

We ran into the same problem in Minneapolis, so Audrey and I went to the newspaper office and asked to speak to the city editor. He gruffly asked, "What do you want?"

"Publicity for our area-wide revival."

"So would all the preachers. What do you have that's newsworthy?"

"A wife," I answered, "who is the world's greatest lady professional magician."

"What can she do that's newsworthy?"

"Drive a car blindfolded, in a car that you select, on streets she has never been on before."

"I don't believe it," he said, "and I am going to make you prove it." He called the Cadillac dealership and arranged for a convertible. Then he asked his best photographer to ride with Audrey, saying, "This preacher and I will wait."

After the usual preparation Audrey was led to the car, and we sat down on a bench to wait. Ten minutes, twenty minutes, twenty-five minutes. Finally Audrey pulled up. Before the city editor could say a word, the photographer yelled that he was going for more film.

When he returned, I asked if we got any publicity.

"Any publicity!" the photographer exclaimed. "This was fantastic. You just got the entire page!"

Sure enough, the entire back page was covered with pictures of Audrey driving blindfolded and the expressions of the people who watched her. One man, coming up from a sewer, saw her and jumped back in. A window washer got so nervous he dropped a bucket of water on the sidewalk below.

The Lord richly blessed the evangelistic meetings Audrey and I conducted as members of the Extension Department of the Moody Bible Institute. In all of our meetings, Audrey conducted special sessions for boys and girls immediately after school. In these meetings, I led the singing, using the choruses the kids enjoyed, and after a rousing song service, Audrey presented her Magic with a Message.

For one meeting Audrey advertised that she would bring her

pet skunk, Pete. We wondered why there was a bottleneck at the door of the church just before the service. As we hurried to the door, we met a mother who demanded, "Where's my daughter, and why did she take all of my clothespins?" Just then she spotted the girl seated at a table, selling clothespins for a nickel each.

"Well," the girl explained, "the Magic Lady said she was going to bring her pet skunk. I thought maybe he might get scared, and he'd . . . he'd . . . well, you know. I thought I could sell clothespins for our noses."

Of course, Pete never got excited—and he never caused a stink!

Another of our meetings was held in a church directly across the street from a theater. Every afternoon we had more kids than the theater did, so the manager came over to see why. He was popular with the kids, and they greeted him as he came in. Audrey asked him to come to the platform and turn his coat pocket inside out. It was empty. She asked one girl to pour flour into a sifter and another to add sugar and other ingredients. Holding the sifter over his pocket, she started turning the crank, much to the kids' delight. After a boy had taken a sip of milk from a glass, she poured the rest of the milk into the pocket. Then she had to cook it. Asking a boy to strike a match, she lit a piece of paper and put that in his pocket also. The kids screamed and the manager started to tremble.

"Reach forth your hand," said the Magic Lady, "and see what you have in your pocket." He did, and to his great surprise, he pulled out a beautiful cake, which he tasted and pronounced delicious.

He asked his assistant to run the theater, and he used his big car every day to bring the kids to the meeting; and one day, he received the Lord Jesus, and gave himself for the work of the Lord.

In every evening service I led the singing and sang a solo before Audrey presented fifteen minutes of magic. Then I preached and gave an invitation. Many came to the Lord.

Audrey's tricks were terrific and drew big crowds. Sometimes she appeared on the platform with a silk. As she waved it around, a bowl of fire appeared. Then a sweep of the hand caused the fire to vanish, replaced with a bowl of flowers. She said, "Eternity, eternity, where will you spend eternity? 'Tis hell or heaven for you and me. Make your choice. Which will it be?" The message burned its way into the hearts and memories of the kids and brought many to salvation.

She used an electric chair, plugged into the church's current, very effectively. She took a torch, dipped it in lighter fluid, and touched the chair, which burst into flames. The pastor sat on the chair and Audrey asked his wife to throw the switch (some of them really enjoyed doing this). Audrey handed him a burned-out fluorescent tube, which would not work in the light fixture, and it glowed brightly in the pastor's hand. Or she lit a torch from his hand.

We were in Oklahoma when we first got the chair, and Audrey was anxious to try it out. She gave me the privilege (??) of being the first, and we went out onto our host-pastor's driveway. It had rained that morning and the drive was still wet. I sat down, and Audrey enthusiastically threw the switch. It was about to fry me. Trying to smile, I said, "Turn it off, dear." She thought I asked her to turn it up—and she obliged. I had amps in my pants. I couldn't sit, and I couldn't get up. Finally she realized that something was wrong, and turned it off, much to my relief.

One pastor got stage fright at the last minute, so his wife bravely volunteered to take his place. We didn't know it, but her corset had metal stays—she got the point. She was not burned, but she was most anxious for the demonstration to end.

This trick illustrated that we will be on fire if there's nothing between our soul and the Savior, in close communion with the Lord, and that our lights will burn brightly for Him who said, "Let your light so shine before men that they may see your good works and glorify your Father which is in heaven."

Newspapers headlined: "Guidos to Display Their Bag of Tricks." Once in Anderson, Indiana, more than four hundred kids overflowed a church sanctuary. Only fifty had been expected, so traffic control was needed.

Nine hundred high school young people were ecstatic

about the performance and pleaded with their principal for more. In both incidents many in attendance, often perennial troublemakers, made their way to the front, kneeling in prayer with Michael and Audrey. Thirty years ago police departments were asking the Guidos to "come and help the kids," in various cities and communities. The police thought that the couple's presentations could be the answer to a "new concern" called juvenile delinquency.

Audrey's repertoire appears unlimited. She smiles and says that she could probably perform for twelve hours and not exhaust her resources.

The basic effects of magic are listed with words that have far deeper meaning to the Sower and his magic lady.

> Attraction! What the gospel should be to those
>   who have never been assured of their eternal
>   destiny
> Identification! Christ in me, the hope of glory
> Thought Transmission! "Let this mind be in you,
>   which is also in Christ"
> Restoration! "Come unto Me ye who labor and are
>   heavy laden and I will give you rest"
> Memorization! What we all need to do with God's
>   word—hide it in our hearts
> Illusion and Disillusion! What this old world has
>   to offer without Christ

They know that only God has the power to transform a life. They rejoice in their special role in God's vineyard. Some do the work of plowing up the fallow ground. Some scatter seeds of God's Word. Some share the benefit of others' harvest. Constantly they are reminded that last year's seeds must be cared for and often planted again. It is good to be reminded that, in the Christian context, it is not the responsibility of the sower to pretest the soil.

How dearly Michael and Audrey wish "everyone" would respond to the message of Jesus. Then they are reminded that cocklebur seeds, a painful nuisance with their sharp, clinging spines, germinate in different years.

Graham Hodges shared with students that "Thus if seed A fails to sprout next year because of a serious drought, another seed, seed B, will be there waiting for another year. Seed C factors into a different year and awaits its conditions for germination to arrive."

So it is with the seeds of ministry. Whether it be magic or applications of chemistry, singing, preaching, writing, or sharing, in the Lord's germination schedule, some seeds will bear fruit. With Him, delay is not denial.

Audrey and Michael have used illusion as a bridge to reality . . . and there is nothing more *real* than a truly changed life.

CHAPTER 8

SOWING IN THE SHADOWS

He who dwells in the secret place of the Most High
Shall abide under the shadow of the Almighty.
I will say of the LORD, "He is my refuge and my fortress;
My God, in Him I will trust."

Psalm 91:1–2

Michael had been speaking and singing for years. Constantly he and Audrey were on the road sharing the Lord without allowing anything to stand in the way of winning the lost.

When he was young in the faith, his mother had made an indelible impression on Michael. She had said, "Son, across every forehead you see, I want you to see the Bible inscription, *'For whom Christ died.'* That will constrain you to witness and to win souls. Now let's pray that the Lord will open your spiritual eyes and allow you to see this on everyone you meet."

The Lord heard her prayer. From that day on when he met people, Michael visualized "For whom Christ died" before he noticed very much else. His mother's words lived as a deeply inbred commission to speak a word, give a tract, or win more souls to the Lord.

SOMETIMES JUST A sentence spoken for Jesus may save a soul from hell. One day I had the joy of leading a tough fellow, Joe, to the Lord. He was a wholesale sinner who made money by breaking the law. I suggested that he get a job.

"What a revolting thought!" he said. "But I'll do it." He found work at the steel plant in Lorain, and on his first day at work he ran into an old friend. "Louie . . ." he began.

"I know," Louie said. "You got religion. I don't want to hear about it. Button your lips."

Joe remembered about that one sentence spoken for Jesus so he shouted as Louie walked away, "Okay. But remember, you got a date with the undertaker." That night he called and said, "Man, did I goof. Wasn't that stupid to tell a friend he had a date with an undertaker?"

"Of course not," I reassured him. "Let's just ask God to bless it." And we prayed.

Early the next morning, Joe phoned and asked me to come to his house. Louie was there and told me about Joe's attempt to witness: "When I walked off yesterday, I couldn't shake what he said about the undertaker. I went to a dance with my sister last night, and she collapsed and died. She's having *her* date with the undertaker. If it'd been me, I'd have been in hell. Help me. I want to be saved." The three of us knelt, and Louie received the Lord Jesus. He went on to Bible school, college and seminary—all because of the timing of one sentence spoken for Jesus.

Often I am asked, "How will I know which sentence to speak?" When we are yielded to the Lord and walk and talk with Him, He'll give us the sentence. A Christ-mastered person can be the master of circumstances.

The unforgiving, evangelistic schedules finally took a toll. At age thirty-one, after completing a campaign in Martinsville, Illinois, Michael suffered a heart attack. Through her many inner concerns Audrey reassured herself in the Lord. Some would have questioned why or asked where God was; the Guidos clung to the Word.

Who among you fears the LORD?
Who obeys the voice of His Servant?
Who walks in darkness

And has no light?
Let him trust in the name of the LORD
And rely upon his God (Isa. 50:10).

Truly they both feared the Lord and practiced daily that faith and obedience were synonymous. The heart attack served as another opportunity to trust the Lord explicitly. They did.

Three years later at the close of a meeting in Phoenix, Arizona, Michael had his second heart attack, and again tried to slow down. It was difficult. But, by God's providence, both attacks came before open dates on the calendar.

The third attack, and most severe, gave the couple an opportunity to live the words of the theme song that opens one of Michael's programs: "Fearing neither clouds nor winter's chilling breeze."

This was a new season in their lives, another circumstance calling for raw faith in the trustworthiness of God. Amidst the chill, they clung to their confidence that spring would appear again.

The doctor tried to scare Michael: "You're going to die."

"Yes, I know," Michael calmly responded. "It is appointed to man once to die and after that, the judgment." He had no fear of the valley of the shadow of death.

Neither blessed nor amused, the doctor told him, "You are going to die *now* unless you start taking better care of yourself."

Those harsh words of warning finally persuaded Michael to go to the Mayo Clinic. Specialists there diagnosed his problem and issued further restrictions: "You should resign from evangelistic work, buy a nice farm, and retire."

The Guidos could not accept this alternative. They had cut the word *retirement* from their personal dictionary years before.

Amazingly, as with the first two attacks, they did not miss a meeting. God again divinely built rest into the usually heavy travel plans.

One specialist gave Audrey a word of hope: "If you can get him through his fiftieth year, he'll probably be all right." And indeed, the specialist was right. Michael enjoyed a joyous seventy-fifth birthday in 1990. *The* Specialist brought His health and healing and an abundance of peace to Michael. And Michael is also quick to credit Audrey for her loving care:

SHE NURSED ME when I was sick, strengthened me when I was weak, cheered me when I was sad, and lifted me when I was low. She even did a number on my inferiority complex!

When I was first saved, some people said to me, "Your parents are Italian. They're poor. Your father can't speak good English. You played for nightclubs and burlesque shows. God can't use you." At low points of my recovery, I was troubled by those remarks.

Patiently and persistently, Audrey pointed to famous Italians who had accomplished great things for Italy, the United States, and the world. Then she recited some of the worst sinners who became the best of saints. She also encouraged my father to be proud of his roots and homeland, reminding all of us that great mathematicians, scientists, musicians, artists, and astronomers had come from that 'old country.'

I was reminded of this when we were invited to the largest church of a great denomination for a one-week revival. On the platform for the first morning service the famous pastor leaned over and asked me for a list of my degrees and graduate schools. My heart sank. I could feel the devil getting ready to give me a knockout blow. I glanced at Audrey. She seemed to sense my problem and gave me a thumbs-up. Lifting a prayer, I confessed I was about to sink. "Lord, help me with an answer."

Looking at the pastor, I said, "Doctor, I didn't bring my thermometer with me; I can't tell you how many degrees I have."

He laughed and said, "You're great! That's what I'll tell the congregation."

Bless the Lord—He kept me from being embarrassed or defeated.

The pastor went on, "I have several university professors with their families. They are highly educated, learned men. I have been trying for a long time to introduce them to the Lord and to bring them into our church. I hope that you will preach something *deep* to interest them."

I thanked him for his suggestion, then I did what I always do—preached a simple message that children can understand and enjoy. I believe if I can interest them, the Holy Spirit will draw the family to Himself.

My sermon was simple, but the Lord blessed it mightily. The professors and their families came forward. Asked the pastor, "What is your secret? Why would a simple message win them?"

I replied, "People go to heaven *heart first*. They go to hell *head first*."

"I think," remarked the pastor, "that I will be changing my messages."

Audrey, too, has had physical problems. But the Great Physician has cared for this team He brought together. He leads and sustains. He gives strength in trials and shadows. Both encourage one another. They communicate extremely well, and never hide one minute item from the other.

Michael says,

SHE KNOWS WHEN I am discouraged and I know when she is. Hopefully, we'll never get discouraged at the same time!

If we ever did, it would be time to remember that awful accident and the vows we made then to the Lord. He alone spared our lives, keeping us "under the shadow of the Almighty." That's when we rededicated ourselves, promising to do the work of not two people but four.

Another shadow for the Guidos was the lack of a child. In her thirties, Audrey questioned the Lord, "What's wrong? We see so many unwanted children." Though some Christians criticized her for not staying home and planning to adopt, she and Michael felt God had called Audrey to work beside her husband. In the years of traveling and being in a church for just a few days at a time, Michael needed the companionship and fellowship of an undivided wife. Audrey had times of feeling she should be at home, but Dr. Will Houghton, Moody's president, wisely assured her that she was called to be with her husband. His view was not popular then. But he, too, had been counseled of the Lord.

Rarely a day passes when the Guidos are not given another opportunity to implicitly *trust* God. They take sincerely Psalm 115:11, "You who fear the LORD, *trust* in the LORD." That trust factor is deeply inbred in them both. They have experienced that God is too wise to err and too good to be unkind to those who love and serve Him. And they pass that message on to the many they minister to each day.

When Michael was hospitalized in Augusta for surgery, that trust was in place. Shortly before he was to be taken to the operating room it was noised around that Michael Guido, the Sower, was just outside the prep room. One by one, doctors, orderlies, nurses, and assistants dropped by to ask, "Would you pray for me?" His proven trust in God became a symbol to others to trust also, and that confidence was dispensed and received as an unexpected blessing to many.

It is easy to coin phrases that symbolize the Sower: Intensive caring is high on the list. Where did it come from?

EVEN WHEN I was a little boy, I had a heart-feeling for people. That feeling grew just a little more when I saw people hurting. I would *feel* it, and I always wanted to help. When I saw somebody being abused or made fun of, my heart saddened. I just naturally took the side of the underdog. Maybe it was because I knew firsthand what it's like to be teased, to be called poor or "dago." Before I was even old enough to go to school, I cringed when I heard someone ridicule my father's English.

Trust also got Audrey and Michael through many disappointments and fears. They have planted personal seeds of an overcoming life in the gardens of their own lives. They consistently, day by day, hour by hour, cultivate faith with prayer. They have never been preoccupied with the past or the future. They are grateful for things they have learned and blessings bestowed. Answers to their prayers are monumental. Yet, *today* is essential. Jesus reminded us not to worry about tomorrow. They realize the past has no future for winning souls and tomorrow has no guarantee, so they work *today!* This attitude has kept them strong through disappointment and risk of harm.

WHEN WE WERE invited to a large church for a meeting, we asked the church to make a motel reservation. We can do a better job for the Lord in the privacy of a motel room. The pastor had a member who owned a large boarding house, and to keep from hurting her feelings, he booked us there.

When we arrived on a cold evening, this woman opened the door and jerked me inside. I protested that my wife was still outside. She opened the door and said, "Hurry up! I can't heat the outside too."

"I need to get my bags."

"Then get 'em!"

We followed her up three flights of stairs into a musty, cobweb-covered room. After she left, Audrey looked around: "I took you for better or worse. This is worse!"

"Cheer up," I consoled her. "At least we have our private bathroom." With that I fastened our newspaper on the walls to cover the dirt, and we hung as few clothes as we could get by with on the nails in the wall. After prayer we fell asleep. I went into the bathroom during the middle of the night, and discovered a woman there, taking a bath.

I looked away and asked, "What are you doing in our bathroom?"

"Your bathroom? This is the only bathroom for three families. We've been parading through your room all night."

We decided to pay the bill at a motel. As we were walking

down the steps, the woman said, "If you leave, I won't come to the meeting."

Getting into the car, I facetiously said to Audrey, "I hope she keeps her word . . . well, not really."

How many times do we neglect our hearts, Christ's home, and shut Him, the very King of Kings, out of life's concerns? We had to learn as traveling evangelists that God expects us to be wise in varying situations and trust Him when we have no control.

Many times we closed a meeting on a Friday night, drove all night and the next day, and opened the next engagement with a gigantic youth rally Saturday night.

On one such occasion we left Michigan and headed for west Texas, driving a station wagon loaded with magic. About two or three in the morning and over a hundred miles from the next city, we noticed a car following closely. There were six men inside. Several times they bumped our car and motioned for us to stop. I floorboarded the old station wagon, but we couldn't outrun them. Then they got ahead of us and blocked the road. I drove around them on the shoulder of the road, calling fervently on the Lord for His protection, claiming "The angel of the Lord encamps 'round them that fear Him and delivers them."

Just as we thought the men would force us to stop, two big trucks, horns honking, passed. The drivers blocked the road with their rigs and ran back wielding baseball bats and tire irons. Pulling the pursuing fellows out of their car, they said, "If you try this again, we'll knock your blocks off. Now get in your car, and don't try that again."

They turned to us and said, "One of us will go in front of you, and the other will get behind you. We'll 'hug' you into the next city. We can report it to the state patrol there."

Just when we needed Him most, the Lord was there, offering peace and protection with a "hug." It was like the story of the little boy who begged his daddy, "Let me drive the car." The father said, "You may, if you let me place my hands over yours."

That is exactly what happened that night. The Father's hands were placed over ours and over the hearts of some very unlikely truckers. Even in the *shadows,* nothing catches God off guard.

When we arrived in the Midwest, the host pastor had a surprising revelation: "I don't believe in the virgin birth of Christ or the inspiration of the Scriptures, but your work has been successful and mine has been a failure. I'd like to study your ministry and see what makes it tick."

What a shock! Before we could recover he added, "You can preach whatever you want to preach, but I hate long sermons."

I smiled and assured him that I never preach more than twenty or twenty-five minutes.

"Good. I'm going to time you. When your twenty minutes are up, I'll raise my hand and expect you to stop."

"Fine, and when people come forward to trust Christ, I'd like to have the privilege of referring them to a church where the Bible is preached."

"That's a deal."

As the meetings continued, we both stuck to our promises. One day the pastor received a phone call from a local doctor: "A man has just had an accident and he's dying. I can't get any other minister to see him. Will you go?"

The pastor consented, then turned to me and said, "I can't tell a dying man to turn over a new leaf or just to assert his manhood. He's too far gone for that. You know what to tell him. Will you come with me?"

We hurried to the hospital, where the doctor met us with, "You'll only have a few minutes with the patient; he won't live longer than that."

"Take over, Guido," the pastor said.

I spoke softly to the dying man, "Sir, Jesus is knocking at the door of your heart. Won't you let Him come in? If you will, pray this simple prayer: 'Lord Jesus, come into my heart.'"

The dying man whispered the prayer; then he summoned his ebbing strength and nearly shouted, "He came in, Mr. Guido! He really came in!"

That pastor dissolved into tears: "I opened my heart to the Lord at the same time. Christ also came into my heart."

That evening's service was like none the church had ever seen or heard before. Their pastor was now a believer.

Experiences like this one sometimes took a more dramatic turn. During World War II some pastors in Charleston, West Virginia, booked the couple up to fifteen times in one day—for seven days. Often the exhausted Guidos reached their hotel past midnight. On one such very late evening,

AUDREY HAD A feeling that something was wrong. When she said, "Let's get out of here!" I talked her out of her "ominous premonition." She shook me vigorously a little while later and insisted again, "We've got to get out of here!" Heavy with sleep, I walked to the window and looked down from our top-floor room to the street.

What I saw snapped me awake—it looked as if the whole block were on fire. We didn't stop to pick up our things—we just ran down the stairs as fast as we could. Outside we moved our car away from the blazing hotel. Then a horrible thought struck me. All my sermons were up there in the room, and I didn't have copies. I told Audrey, "I've got to go back and get them."

Audrey begged, "Please don't go! You'll never get out alive!"

But I had to try. I promised to be careful and hurried back to the burning building. On my way up the stairs, I woke up several families that hadn't heard the alarm. They were able to get out alive.

Outside Audrey began to cry as she told a firefighter, "My husband is up there."

The firefighter looked doubtful: "Unless the wind changes, he won't get out alive." In his words, Audrey heard the echo of her own words of a few minutes before.

She began to pray, and even as she prayed she felt a shift in the wind. Moments later I rejoined her, holding in my hands my sermon notes—and several pairs of Audrey's new stockings.

Early the next morning I called my mother. She said, "It was the strangest thing. About midnight I woke up with an urgent burden to pray for you and Audrey."

Jesus never fails. He is the refuge, the fortress. "He is *my* God. In Him will I trust." Yes, Jesus can do everything—but fail.

Life has not always been easy in Metter, Georgia, or in the ministry. Yet in all the growth and expansion, the Guidos are convinced that God is on the corner before they arrive: "Before you call, I answer."

There is a story of a very sick man whose wife called in a specialist and asked tearfully if there was any hope. The doctor replied, "It all depends on what you're hoping for." Everyone, including the Sower and his lady, hopes for health and happiness. No one hopes for sickness or suffering. Yet Michael and Audrey know that human life is frail, but God is their refuge and strength. With the psalmist they pray:

> LORD, make me to know my end,
> And what is the measure of my days,
> That I may know how frail I am (Ps. 39:4).

During times of testing, the question may slip into one's consciousness, "Why? Does God know? If He knows, does He care?"

God does know and He does care. For He became man, a real man, who knew our passions, experienced our temptations, and felt our pains. That's why in James 5:13 He spoke: "Is anyone among you suffering? Let him pray." James 5:16 continues, "The effective, fervent prayer of a righteous man avails much."

Michael and Audrey have seen prayer's power in illness, walking close to the shadow of death during an accident and three heart attacks. They have experienced the "hug" of the waiting Father, and His presence has brought them security.

You cannot bring a burden too heavy for God to lift or a problem too hard for Him to solve or a request too big for Him to answer.

God does things no one else can do. He asks in Genesis 18:14, "Is anything too hard for the LORD?"

> Don't worry about anything; instead, pray about
> everything; tell God your needs and don't forget

to thank him for his answers. If you do this you will experience God's peace, which is far more wonderful than the human mind can understand. His peace will keep your thoughts and your hearts quiet and at rest as you trust in Christ Jesus (Phil. 4:6-7 TLB).

CHAPTER 9

*B*Y AND
BY THE
HARVEST

Jesus said to them, "My food is to do the will of Him who sent Me, and to finish His work. Do you not say, 'There are still four months and then comes the harvest'? Behold, I say to you, lift up your eyes and look at the fields, for they are already white for harvest! And he who reaps receives wages, and gathers fruit for eternal life, that both he who sows and he who reaps may rejoice together."

John 4:34–36

The summer Michael and his friend were digging ditches in the cemetery, or "dig-ditching" as they called it, they traded that job for high aspirations to promote their own band. After his total surrender to the Lord, the band, having been "disbanded," still weighed heavily on Michael's heart.

Before leaving the group, he had shared the good news with each one. Some responded favorably, saying it was okay for him, but the pianist was adamant: "Don't bother me, Guido, I'm getting a kick out of life."

"Yes, but it will kick back one of these days," Michael told him. The disinterested pianist continued in his errant ways.

Through the years Michael and Audrey continued to pray for the band members. An answer was on the horizon and drew nearer when they were invited to conduct an areawide revival in the suburbs of

Minneapolis. Nostalgia is written on the faces of the
Sower and his lady as he brings the incident to mind:

ON THE SATURDAY before the meeting started on Sunday, we
drove up to the big tent and walked over to the crusade leaders.
We wondered why they seemed so cold. Then it came out. Finally someone asked, "What kind of company do you keep?"

Joking, I answered, "I'm not particular. I'm here with you."
That was about as stimulating as a hearse.

Another one chimed in, "About an hour ago a big Lincoln
pulled up and some show people got out looking for you. The
fellow said he was a good friend of yours—said they were playing
at a nightclub here where his wife does a striptease and he plays
the drums. That was a real shock for us. We're wondering just
what kind of evangelist we have scheduled."

I must confess that I really didn't blame them, but I was
crushed. This was the first time in my ministry that our paths
crossed with this man who used to play in my band. For years I
had been praying for Bud—ever since I led him into that sort of
business. He had become a famous drummer, billed as "The
Doctor of Drumology." But he had gone deeper into sin. How
Audrey and I thanked God we were in Minneapolis at the same
time Bud and Diane were. We just kept calling all the nightclubs
until we finally located them.

We had a lovely apartment, with a kitchen, reserved for us at a
hotel. Bud and Diane could not come to the services—they were
performing then, and since they slept during the day, we invited
them to the apartment after their shows. Audrey's a wonderful
cook, so she prepared delicious dinners; and we ate and talked
about our show business days together. We did our best to interest them in the Lord and His Word.

Diane was also a medium who held seances, and she did her
striptease act making love to a whiskey bottle. She frightened
us with tales of some of her hair-raising experiences. Praying that
we could get to their hearts by way of their stomachs, Audrey
went all out on exquisite meals. One morning we were thrilled
when they promised to come to the three o'clock Sunday meeting.

The Puritans said, "When you pray, move your feet." We put feet to our prayers by making all the necessary arrangements for them to attend. As the meeting got underway, they were still absent, and we were disappointed.

How thankful we were to see them come in just before Audrey presented her Magic with a Message, which fascinated them. I could see that her message fastened itself to their hearts. All the time I preached, I kept asking God to save Bud and Diane. When the invitation was given, Diane came forward. As she walked down the sawdust aisle, unpinning her hair, which had been twisted into a knot, we were all crying. Joining Audrey at the altar, face awash with tears, she asked the Lord to come into her heart. And He did just as He said He would in Revelation 3:20. As she threw back her head, the sun streaming down on her, those tears sparkled like diamonds. We felt the nail-pierced hand of our Lord come and wipe away her hardness. It was a beautiful sight. Then Bud came, dropped to his knees, and confessed his sins. I could almost hear the Lord say, "Loose him, and let him go!" Thank God! One of my dance band had come to Jesus.

They came to the service that night and gave their heart-stirring testimonies. Bud and Diane canceled their nightclub contract. Bud knew no other trade, but he could use his hands and said he would do anything. He asked us to help him get a job. One of the Christian men hired him to paint. Diane looked forward to writing poems for a greeting card company. Thank God for laymen who help babes in Christ.

The Lord has been pleased to bless our evangelistic crusades. In going into our meetings Audrey and I desired only to be profitable to our Christ and the churches we served. We went to the meetings not to be ministered unto, but to minister; not only to preach, but also to do personal work. We prayed, "Dear Lord, if the time ever comes when we fail to save souls, kill us and take us home to heaven. We don't want to live if we're not soul-winners."

In a big church in Michigan the crowds came, but souls were not being saved. We don't blame others when that happens; we blame ourselves. We don't scold the saints; we search our souls. In this meeting, preaching was like shooting peas at battleships. Night after night we went to our hotel room and spent the rest of the night in prayer, asking, "What is wrong with me?"

One morning about 2:00 the phone rang, and the pastor said, "You answered too quickly to have been asleep. You were praying, weren't you? And you were blaming yourselves. It's not you," he continued. "We're to blame. Go to sleep. After you preach tonight, please let me say a word."

That night after I preached, I turned the meeting over to the pastor. He said, "The Lord has blessed our hearts through the ministry of the Guidos. Because we have not experienced revival, they have been blaming themselves. It's not their fault; it's ours. We are proud of our orthodoxy, proud of membership, proud of Bible knowledge, proud of our abilities; we're even proud of our humility. Pride is standing in the way of a revival." Falling to his knees, he cried, "O God, save us from our pride. Forgive us. We humble ourselves in Thy sight. Have mercy on us, in the name of Jesus."

All the church members went down on their knees. Silently and solemnly they confessed their sins. What a time of crying and cleansing! Then the pastor returned the service to me. The Lord blessed with a harvest of souls.

The salvation of a soul isn't a solo; it's a symphony. When souls are saved in our crusades I feel it's because of the praying and preaching of the pastor, the teaching and travailing of the Sunday school teachers, the supplication and soul-winning of the saved. We always give thanks to the pastor and his people—and the glory to God.

After Bud and Diane professed their conversions, Bud shouted, "Three cheers for Jesus!"

Strange? Not really. He was thinking about the three cheers of our Lord.

First, the cheer of forgiveness. Our Lord said, "Be of good cheer; thy sins be forgiven thee."

Second, the cheer of fellowship. He said, "Be of good cheer; it is I; be not afraid."

Third, the cheer of freedom. He said, "Be of good cheer; I have overcome the world."

Michael and Audrey Guido at the groundbreaking for the
Guido Evangelistic Association in 1962.

Ninth-grade Michael, outfitted for the Lorain High School band.

Young Michael Guido displays his mischievous personality, striking a pose far beyond his five years of age.

Michael at high-school graduation, 1932.

Through more than twenty years of ministry—traveling with evangelists, Michael's pastoring a church, and managing the Association in Metter—the Guidos have made a beautiful team.

Before she met Michael, Audrey taught high-school English and planned to attend Johns Hopkins medical school. Commitment to Michael altered her plans.

Visitors to the Association and members of the community come to the garden chapel, open twenty-four hours a day, to pray and meditate.

The Guido gardens offer visitors a place for quiet reflection and solitude.

Michael stands in front of a painting of "The Sower," which is a stained glass window placed at the Moody Bible Institute in 1889. Michael's memory of his first glimpse of the window has inspired him in his years of work as a "sower."

The Guidos' Norwegian elkhound, Gea—named for Guido Evangelistic Association—has been a faithful friend and a fair assistant as Michael sometimes uses him to make a point when he is on camera.

The Guidos are at home in their work and with one another.

Audrey's knowledge of chemistry enabled her to create illusions that demonstrated important Bible truths.

Audrey drives blindfolded through Orange, Texas. Audrey's antics and demonstrations always managed to draw a crowd and, ultimately, to draw them to God.

*Dena Fowler, television
operations manager*

*Sue Williams, radio
operations manager*

Lila Williams, executive secretary

*The staff of the Guido Evangelistic Association help create an ordered
organization and enable the Guidos to reach the hearts
of people around the world.*

Members of the Association's board of directors.

What destroys happiness? A sense of being forlorn, of being forsaken, and failure.

Three cheers! Our Lord brings the answer to all three.

Michael's prayer for these two new converts is meaningful for us all.

Father, grant that in these strange and strenuous days we may never lose heart or hope. Give us Thy holiness, holiness that makes for happiness. Thy graciousness that leads to contagiousness. Thy sturdiness that leads to faithfulness in Christ. Amen.

During Michael's years at Moody he had practical experiences in jails, missions, and street meetings. Those years increased his passion for souls.

He tells about an experience at Cook County Jail, where he encountered some rough and tough characters when he went every Sunday morning. In one cell block he discovered mean, belligerent inmates.

I WAS ALMOST persuaded to turn around and leave. Following God's leading, I stepped back and started to sing *O Sole Mio*.

To my surprise, this ringleader was an Italian. He applauded when I finished and I confirmed that I, too, was Italian. "Okay, guys," he said to the other prisoners. "I like this kid. We're gonna have church. Listen to him, or I'll knock your block off."

I preached, they listened, and when I gave the invitation, nearly every one professed conversion. When the meeting was over, the ringleader pointed to some buckets of hot water which had been set up to be thrown on the preacher. "I'm glad we didn't," the new convert said. "Will you forgive me?"

With the teachers at Moody fanning the Word of the Lord that burned in my heart, I slipped out of my room every evening to conduct four or five street meetings. One night some ruffians came up. One said, "I like your black, curly hair," as another started pulling it.

Another told me I would make a good punching bag and demonstrated his point. A third one warned me to leave and not come back.

The next night another student, Joe Cellini, a gangster before his conversion, went with me. The three were waiting. I introduced Joe, who looked like a prize-fighter.

Joe said, "Show me the guys who beat you up." I pointed to one, and Joe yanked him up. "Kneel!" Joe commanded.

"I ain't gonna pray," shouted the tough guy.

"I don't expect you to," said Joe. "Kneel." Joe opened his Bible to Proverbs 30:33. "Read it."

As the fellow read aloud, "For as the churning of milk produces butter, and as wringing the nose produces blood . . ." Joe illustrated the literal meaning of the verse.

"The Bible's true, ain't it?" he asked.

He got a sheepish yes in response, and they never threatened me again.

At a service in a Texas prison the Lord allowed His harvest; prisoners were converted and their lives dramatically changed. It was a blessing.

Because the results were so startling and so profitable to the prison system, we were invited to the prison at Huntsville for a service. The prisoners marched in, and Audrey was presenting her magic when the warden said, "Guido, I hear you can sing. My boys love music. Please sing a solo." He brushed aside my protest that I had no music by assuring me that one of his boys could play anything if he heard a few bars of the melody.

Walking over to the curly-haired inmate sitting at the piano with his back to me, I said, "Curly, the warden wants me to sing, but I don't have any music. Will you listen to this tune and play it for me?"

As I started to hum, the pianist jumped off the bench, and threw his arms around me, saying, "Michael, remember me? I'm the piano player from your old band. Now you're a preacher and I'm a prisoner. When you asked me to become a Christian, I told you I was too young to give up the world—I wanted to have some kicks. You warned me that life was going to kick me back—

well, it sure did." How he cried. He played for my solo, and after
the magic, I sang and preached. God blessed in a most wonderful, heart-moving way. Many came forward, and leading the
procession was my old piano player. He was happy; I was happier; but his mother was the happiest of all. On hearing the good
news she wrote and thanked me. Heaven came down and
flooded her heart and home with happiness.

> He breaks the power of canceled sin,
> He sets the prisoner free;
> His blood can make the foulest clean;
> His blood availed for me. (Charles Wesley)

Mr. Shannon instilled in me a love for leading men to the
Lord. "Iron sharpens iron, so one man sharpens another"
(Prov. 27:17 NIV), and Mr. Shannon was masterful at that work.
I had prayed God would grant me that gift. That's why I enjoyed
the prisons and any opportunity to witness to the people in the
military.

The work with members of the armed forces was exciting,
fruitful, and tiring. One day at Camp McCoy, Wisconsin, word
came to the chaplains that their men would be sent overseas immediately. They asked me to speak to all who would be going.
The meetings were arranged: At each I sang a solo and preached
a sermon. Then I gave a New Testament to everyone who said he
would read it. On one day I sang thirty-three solos, preached
thirty-three sermons and handed out hundreds of New Testaments. Many responded to Jesus.

Before I married Audrey, my sister Roxie joined Mr. Shannon
and me at some army bases. We arrived one afternoon at Fort
Benning, Georgia, and went to the large building where the
meeting was scheduled. On one side of the divided structure was
a canteen full of soldiers. The side of our meeting place was
empty. We started our service with Roxie at the piano and my
singing. Our facilities were overflowing as the men brought their
beer over from the canteen, which was soon deserted. They
sipped as I sang. Before long the beers were laid aside as they
came forward and confessed Christ. Like the woman at the well

who left her water pot, they left their beer on the floor and walked out, rejoicing in their Savior.

At some camps and embarkation points, I was scheduled between reels of a movie in the theater, after a show, or at a dance. That's where I reached so many vulnerable, frightened, but brave soldiers, sailors, and marines.

We found a big dance in progress at the service club at Camp Blanding, Florida, one evening. I asked the hostess for permission to hold a service after the dance. In love with the Lord and anxious for the men to be saved, she consented, but she declined to introduce me. After the dance Roxie hurried to the piano, and she made it talk! Everyone applauded loudly. Then I stepped up and started singing some easy-listening songs. They joined in one.

In a split second the Lord showed me how to introduce Mr. Shannon. "Fellows," I suggested, "Let's sing 'The Old Gray Mare Ain't What She Used to Be.'" They sang it lustily. "I'm going to dedicate that song to my old buddy," I said. "While he was mayor of his hometown, he owned a liquor store, and he was his own best customer. But he got converted, and the ole mayor ain't what he used to be." They applauded wildly. Mr. Shannon spoke briefly but inspiringly. That night we gave out hundreds of New Testaments, and many came to the Lord.

I'll never forget one commanding officer who arrogantly said to me, "My men don't need Christ. What they need is wine, women, and cigarettes. But come back at three o'clock and we'll talk about it."

Later in the day a young man we had led to the Lord was accidentally shot and lay dying. He said to the chaplain, "Please write my mother and tell her I died trusting Christ and that I'll meet her in heaven."

My coworker in the camps asked the commanding officer, "Colonel, how would you comfort that mother? Would you tell her to be of good cheer—that we had given her boy wine to drink until he couldn't swallow another drop; that we gave him women to enjoy until he closed his eyes in death; that we gave him cigarettes to smoke until he couldn't draw another breath? Is this how you would comfort that brokenhearted mother?"

"Gentlemen," he admitted, "I was wrong. I will give you my car. I'll drive, if need be. But we will take you to every man under my command so you can present Christ to them. That's what we all need."

To those military people, Michael often repeated his spiritual alphabet. Christ is our

> Advocate to intercede
> Blesser to imburse
> Companion to sympathize
> Deliverer to free
> Eternal Life to enjoy
> Friend to cheer
> Guard to protect
> Helper to sustain
> Inheritance to satisfy
> Joy to delight
> King to serve
> Leader to follow
> Mediator to interpose
> Nourishment to support
> Offering to propitiate
> Power to keep
> Quietness to soothe
> Rock to shelter
> Shepherd to lead
> Treasurer to enrich
> Understanding to illumine
> Vanguard to establish
> Way to God.

Each of these experiences reveals Michael's suggestions on how to capture someone's attention and witness to the Lord's love. After all, Jesus Christ was a man's man, King of Kings, Lord of Lords, the Master revolutionary who turned the world right side up.

Still, in the 1990s, Michael continues to work with and

minister to service people. Various camps, posts, training centers, and military hospitals use him to encourage the personnel and make space for Sower booklets in recreation and reading areas.

A young serviceman from the South had been raised on a peanut plantation. Lonely and discouraged during his first weeks of basic training, he sat on his bunk watching another G.I. read and keep saying, "What about that! What about that!"

"What about *what?*" cautiously asked the lonely soldier. To which the reply came, "What about George Washington Carver!" And he proceeded to read a portion from one of the *Sower* publications:

> George Washington Carver was an American who was born a slave, but whose research as an agricultural chemist won him international fame. In his laboratory, Carver prayed for wisdom whereby the peanut might be put to new use, and he made over three hundred products from the peanut. He was invited to testify before a Senate Committee, and there he was asked, "Dr. Carver, how did you learn all these things?" He replied, "From an old Book." "What book?" asked the chairman. "The Bible," he said. "Does the Bible talk about peanuts?" asked the senator. "No, Mr. Senator," he replied, "but it tells about the God who made the peanut. I asked Him to show me what to do with the peanut, and He did."

The two men looked at each other in wonder. Both had come from peanut plantations. Neither had heard of George Washington Carver. Both had in their possessions New Testaments from the Pocket Testament League.

Coincidence or providence? More than forty years ago, Michael worked with service people through Pocket Testament League. Today he continues to share with them. These two military men became friends. The booklet encouraged them and they were challenged to ask God to "show them what to do with their lives." Through the local base chaplain, they started planting and spreading their personal seeds of faith.

God delights in those who plant and water seeds. He also delights in those who keep planting and keep watering.

> And let us not grow weary while doing good, for in due season we shall reap if we do not lose heart. Therefore, as we have opportunity, let us do good to all, especially to those who are of the household of faith (Gal. 6:9,10).

Along the Christian way it is easy to grow weary in well doing or to stop short and become distracted. The harvest comes from those who have a will to "finish His work," to faithfully "stir up the gift that is in [them] . . . run with faith and endurance . . . and finish the course."

The Sower continues to define and to live what it means to follow Christ. Won't you accept the challenge to win those on your block, in your sphere of influence, and in your home? Daily plant seeds of faith and love so . . .

> By and by the harvest
> And the labor ended
> We shall come rejoicing,
> Bringing in the sheaves.

PART THREE

CHAPTER 10

GOING
FORTH
WITH
WEEPING

Those who sow in tears
Shall reap in joy.

Weeping may endure for a night,
but joy comes in the morning.

Psalms 126:5; 30:5

A storm, with blinding flashes of lightning and deafening crashes of thunder, frightened a little girl who cried, "Mama, come!"

Running to her daughter, the mother said, "Don't be afraid. God is near."

"I know He is," replied the girl, "but when the storm's bad, I want someone with skin on them."

That is where God's people come in. God is looking for men and women who will find a burden and bear it, a hurt and heal it, a scarcity and supply it. Christians are called to befriend the friendless, help the helpless, and offer prayers for the prayerless. People need more than affection and sympathy—there must be action.

The Guidos are committed to the belief that if you care, you will share. Multitudes of people have been the recipients of their unselfish availability.

ONE MORNING THE phone rang at 4:30. A voice from a distant city said, "Hello. I play for a rock group. I am sexed out, doped out, and drunk out. I've tried everything, but life is just a big soap bubble. Now I don't even want to live."

I could hear weeping in his voice as he continued, "I called my mother about an hour ago and told her I was going to kill myself. She begged me not to and told me to get right with God instead. She told me that before I do anything drastic I should see your one-minute telecast. Just to please her I promised I would."

I was intent on the need at the other end of the line. The caller continued, "I just saw you on television, and what you said gave me hope. I need help. What should I do?"

"Come to the Lord Jesus just as you are. Receive Him, believe Him, turn from all your sins, and then live for Him."

Again he wept; "I will." There was now determination in his voice. "Dear Jesus, I turn from my sins, all my sins. I want You to come into my heart and life and save me. Please come in *now*." Seconds later he exclaimed, "He did come in, Mr. Guido! I'm saved. Please excuse me, but I have to hang up and call my mother."

Many callers are heartened and surprised that I answer the telephone. One morning, I said, as I always do, "Hello, and good morning—the Sower."

After a moment's hesitation a lady asked, "With whom am I speaking?" Her speech and language revealed a woman of culture.

"Michael Guido."

"Oh, I didn't think *you* would be answering the phone at this hour of the morning. I'm amazed."

"Ma'am, I feel when you call at this hour, you need help. How may I help you?"

"My husband came home with a prostitute last night. I was so hurt and angry that I wanted to kill both of them. As I went to get my pistol, I turned on the television to drown out the noise of the shot I intended to fire. Your program was on, and your message stopped me in my tracks. After I heard you, a wonderful thing transpired. I put the gun down and asked Christ to save me and take control of my life and heart.

"Magnificently, it happened," she continued. "He did save me, and my attitude is different. I don't want to kill my husband and that girl; I want them to be saved too. Will you please pray for them and for me?"

You just can't beat the Lord!

> These stories pour from the heart of the Sower and his lady, both keenly aware that heartbreaks and needs of people will interrupt their sleep again and again. Their motivation? For the frightened, needy, desperate caller, they *know* that Jesus is the answer. And for those callers the weeping of the night is only the prelude to joy in the morning.

DURING A CRUSADE in Waycross, Georgia, as I walked from my hotel to the church nearby, I passed a woman who did a double take, her face revealing recognition. "Mr. Guido, you don't know me, but last week I decided to take my life. After I poured poison into a cup, I turned on the television and sat down to die. Then I heard the melodious sound of your birds singing. I looked up. There you were on the screen, talking about kindness, happiness, and peace—all the things I was longing for.

"I put down my cup of death to look and listen intently. You convinced me in just that brief moment that I needed Jesus. I received Him into my heart as best as I knew how to. Wonder of wonders, He saved me. I wanted to say thank you . . . thank you more than you will ever comprehend."

One night a woman called me from sleep and said, "I'm dying. I just overdosed. I saw your telecast and I wanted to know more in these last minutes of life. Can you help me?"

I tried in vain to get the caller to give her name, but she kept asking for prayer. I told her I wanted to pray for her specifically, but she still wouldn't identify herself.

Audrey picked up another phone and listened for any clue that would be an opening to call the hospital or an emergency number. This time it didn't work. For a moment there was a flicker of hope, but it went out forever. The voice faded into the night. We still wonder whether that caller went to everlasting darkness or to the light of God's presence. That's what keeps us answering those phones even though it takes a physical, emotional, and personal toll.

Sometimes we are threatened or suspect danger from a local caller. Law enforcement here responds quickly and willingly. One evening while we were talking with friends, I remarked that I was amazed how often the police would be nearby when I reached the home of a desperate, needy caller who had asked for help.

A concerned, knowing look took over Audrey's beautiful face, and she finally confessed her secret. Whenever she felt I was headed into danger, she quietly alerted the police. That evening the magic lady unlocked a mystery which had plagued me for years. I just thank the Lord for a wife who is a loving prayer partner, but who also puts a "policeman's feet" to some of her prayers.

The law enforcement people in Metter are a cadre of caring individuals. Two sitting near the call boards were asked what influence the Sower had in his hometown. It was delightful to listen to the officer respectfully say that if it weren't for Michael, Metter would not be known. The thousands of visitors who come into the city each month help commerce and have a very positive influence on the citizens. He eagerly related that what the Guido Evangelistic Association represents to the county and state is easily measured in its curbing of crime and drug traffic.

He was aware of the many who use Michael for a sounding board or who bring their problems to him. All age groups respond to Michael. The officer was also impressed, in a day when TV evangelists have fallen, that Michael does not even own an automobile. "They give so much away to people in need, especially in their hometown." Metter's officers have good reasons for taking care of the Guidos.

ONE CALL CAME on a typical morning. The officer said, "An armed man, who's out to kill two cops, may be headed your way. When he phoned, he mentioned the possibility of coming by to see you because he watches you on TV. We'll patrol the area, but be on the lookout."

Thanks to the warning, I was alerted to the sound of the car stopping. I went right outside and saw a pistol and several shells spill onto the parking area as the driver opened the car door. "I'm about to do something terrible," the fugitive said. "Help me so I won't kill anybody."

I led him into the studio office, opened my Bible, and began to read. That nervous man listened intently, absorbing every word. After only a few moments, he responded to the Word that became flesh, and Jesus Christ came into his heart. I equipped him with some kind advice and booklets before he returned to the authorities, his life changed.

The police department reacted to yet another miracle on Lewis Street. Said one sergeant, "Those several acres are witness to the incredible all the time. Our work is sure made easier. Those people [the Guidos] can be completely trusted in all situations. What a couple! Amazing! Amazing!"

When told of the sergeant's words, Michael protested, "Not what a couple—what a God!"

The love of God continues to constrain these indomitable workers. Increased social contacts have a stimulating effect on their hearts and personalities, best described from the wisdom of Solomon:

As in water face reveals face,
So a man's heart reveals the man (Prov. 27:19).

Some of the calls that tug the heaviest on personal emotions are the ones from children. There are many and they increase yearly.

Latchkey kids, children home alone, often before and after school, make a growing portion of calls to the Sower. Life for them is frightening—and with good reason.

Grade-school-age latchkey kids live in loneliness and are very prone to accidents. By the time the youngsters approach eighth grade, the risk of drugs and alcohol looms. Some are exposed much earlier. A nine-year-old boy told us, "I drink 'cuz my parents could care less. I'm really nobody's child."

With the lack of after-school care and the proliferation of one-parent homes, kids feel isolated; in their young minds they see themselves as "disposable commodities." Like the little girl afraid of thunder, they all seek someone with skin on, someone who cares and will listen.

We must remember there is no 800 number or telephone number of any kind given at the end of the Sower's broadcasts—just Metter, Georgia. Therefore these youngsters must think of how to obtain the number first. Many of these children call long distance.

TO MONITOR CALLS, we had the telephone company install a machine that lets us know where the calls come from, how many per hour, and the specific times. The numbers are significantly higher during the pre- and after-school hours.

Once a child called right from home base in Metter. The little one felt encouraged, and Audrey invited her to visit sometime. She does. Many neighborhood children come to the chapel— some before school, some after, and some both times. The school-age children often are in the chapel in the morning, kneeling and then rushing off to catch the school bus whose driver is patiently waiting. The kids know Audrey and I are their friends. Age is no barrier.

One call came in the night. The young girl was alone. She said that her dad was an undertaker and she was frightened to be home alone. "We have two bodies here, and I'm literally scared to death. Will you help me? I just wish I could have someone here with me right now."

Her voice calmed as Michael reassured her, "I know how you can have somebody with you, and He will be delighted to stay with you and protect you. It's Jesus. He has a word just for you. 'Behold, I stand at the door and knock. If anyone hears My voice and opens the door, I will come in to him and dine with him, and he with Me'" (Rev. 3:20).

I carefully explained that the door was the door to her heart. The person knocking was Jesus. If she wanted to let Him into her heart and life, the latch was on the inside of her will.

I then asked her, "Would you like to ask Jesus to come in and then be with you wherever you are?"

"I would." After praying she spoke confidently, "He's in my heart and right in this very room. Thank you. Good-bye."

Just before dawn, she called back. "I'm still not afraid or scared. I want to thank you. May I come and see you?" She came at about 9:00. It was a joyous time to reassure her. Today she is faithfully serving the Lord.

Children have fears difficult for us to comprehend. They call about Dad being drunk and hitting Mom, about Mom having a boyfriend, about having no food or medicine [an item the Guidos respond to regularly]. Others fear the breakdown of the ozone layer, wondering if the greenhouse effect is growing death for the universe or wondering about "environmental impact." They're scared about drugs and want to say no. They confess to being abused and act like their confidence has been permanently poisoned.

Even the tiny ones fear nuclear bombs. Somebody recently said that since most preachers no longer predict the end of the world, teachers have taken their place and embraced the message of doom, which alarms the kids.

Michael and Audrey have the fine and gentle art of lifting those children to God. They love them dearly. And that love, like wonderful ribbons, becomes a tie that binds these needy young ones to the loving spirits of the Sower and his lady.

An abused, lonely nine-year-old girl, victim of racial slurs and parental dissension, describes it best: "The Sower showed me how Jesus wanted to wrap me in the ribbon of His love. And a 'purty' ribbon it is."

A budding young gardener, aged six, was helping Mom in the garden. Watering a beautiful plant she exclaimed, "Mom, I know why flowers grow!"

"Why?"

"Because they want to get out of the dirt."

Children of God, whatever their age, have their roots on earth, but hearts set on things above. The cues for behavior, confidence, faith, and hope come from the Word, not the world.

THE BEST WAY TO LIVE IN THIS WORLD IS TO LIVE ABOVE IT

ONE TEENAGE GIRL phoned me and said, "I'm as crooked as a dog's leg and bad as hell. I've had one abortion and I want another. Please help me get it."

"You're on drugs too, aren't you?" I asked, hearing the slurring in her voice. "Your arm is like a human pin cushion." When she admitted to being hooked on cocaine, I went on: "You're not proud of the sins you've committed. You don't want to add to the list by killing your child, do you?"

She started to cry and said she had never thought of it like that before. She asked the Lord to come into her heart, and we found a home for her until the baby, which she planned to give up, was born. She changed her mind and came to see me, bringing that beautiful baby with her. She told me she really did love the child's father. At my suggestion, she brought him in. After he received the Lord, they married in the chapel, the two of them cradling their child. Both of them are very happy.

Said a listener who was influenced for good and whose little child found the Lord through telephone calls on the Metter lines, "I've never met that Sower. But I'm convinced of something my grandma taught me. A lesson I need to pull out and restudy, a lesson those 'minute messengers' know well: *You can give without loving, but not love without giving.*"

She continued, "I describe myself as a 'toxic parent.' I kept telling the kids they were bad and worthless. I taught them to lie for me and steal for my habit. My legacy to the kids was worthless. In the midst of all this conflict and hatefulness, the seeds from the radio and boob tube

grew like flowers in uncultivated ground. Seeds of
believing in people, praying for your mother, talking to
God about everything. We are changed! Really changed!"

IN ONE OF our meetings, a boy in a wheelchair made his way
down the aisle. "He's too young," his mother protested. The
father said, "Leave him alone. Maybe he has to do this in order
to feel better about himself."

It was Christmastime and I had preached on "the gift of God,
which is eternal life." The boy wanted the gift. He received it as
a child. Trusting. Believing. Responding.

Jesus Christ is an equal opportunity Savior. The children of
men are equally in need of His redemptive work, and all must
come as children—if not in age, then in spirit.

The calls keep coming in. The weeping expresses the
sadness and feelings of helplessness the callers relate.

Thank God, Audrey and Michael and their dedicated
staff bring "joy in the morning" as they faithfully keep
"sowing for the Master."

CHAPTER 11

SOWING FOR THE MASTER

He who sows sparingly will also reap sparingly, and he who sows bountifully will also reap bountifully. So let each one give as he purposes in his heart, not grudgingly or of necessity; for God loves a cheerful giver.

2 Corinthians 9:6–7

And I heard the voice of the LORD walking in the garden. . . .

Genesis 3:8

Guido Gardens is a tranquil corner in a rural American setting. Sparkling waterfalls, shimmering fountains and babbling brooks, gazebos, and a uniquely crafted prayer chapel beautify the grounds on which the Sower's telecasts are produced.

ONE MORNING THE manager of a visiting carnival and his wife visited our gardens and studio. They were in town for only a week and had just suffered the loss of a loved one. They needed someone to talk to. The quietness of these acres brought them a sense of peace they had not felt in years.

I listened and wept with them. We prayed together. "We're not used to anybody wanting to talk to 'carney' people," they said. "We're so grateful." And they responded to the gospel.

Walking through the garden they asked, "Where's the white bench we see in your television spots?" I explained that the bench had been borrowed for a TV shoot and had been returned that same afternoon. After the couple left, a Metter store delivered a white bench and several chairs. A gift from the carnival people!

Later on a savage thunderstorm threatened the safety of the carnival, performers and townspeople. That couple came back and asked me to pray for them. I followed them down to the carnival site. After they secured the rides and shut up the booths, the manager announced over the loudspeakers, "Please stand by, friends. Reverend Michael Guido, the Sower, will lead us in prayer." I asked the Lord to protect the people and the property, and God answered. That prayer appeared later in the magazine for carnival people with a testimony to its effectiveness.

Videotaping in the gardens is always an event. The community cooperates; the Rotarians, local friends, and the Bob Quattlebaums from Savannah help furnish food for the crews brought in from network and video production organizations. Audrey cooks her special delicacies, and Michael unveils the fruit of his preparation with newly written scripts for minute messages—all 175 of them!

Again, it is a time to exercise faith. God alone provides for the finances. Audrey and Michael trust His wisdom to manage production.

PRODUCING A TELECAST, even a short one, is a big undertaking. It takes extra praying, planning, and plugging. I write the script, as I do for our four daily broadcasts, our devotionals, and our sermons. Then I memorize them for the videotaping. Audrey is in charge of all business, and she checks around to see who has the best equipment and will give the best shoot for the money before she hires the crew and the company. Then she selects the camera people, the engineers, the audio and tape people, the floor director, and the director. The company she often selects has a fifty-five-foot truck with about $2 million worth of equipment. Sometimes the crew comes with the truck, and sometimes it doesn't. She also selects the sites for the taping. Audrey reserves rooms for the crew at a local motel. To economize, she prepares and serves the crew and staff three meals a day, and she does a superb job. Everyone wants to come back because of the choice meals. *And* she sits in the truck with the director/producer, Dale Hill, serving as the executive producer.

We rise about 4:30 A.M. during the shoot, and while Audrey fixes breakfast, I go over the messages for the day. She serves from about 6:00 to about 7:00.

We do five programs at a time. While the camera crew changes sites, I run into the house and change clothes. Audrey runs from the truck, jumps into her golf cart, and hurries to the house to help me with the clothes she has selected for each site. Then we head right back to our positions to tape the next five. We do fifty to seventy-five programs a day. When we first started, the crew asked Audrey how many we intended to complete in one day. When she told them fifty or sixty, they corrected her: "You mean five or six, don't you? They don't make any more than that in Hollywood."

Audrey reminded them that we don't have the money Hollywood has: "We do our best to redeem the time. We make every minute count for the Lord."

After the shoot, the crew told her that they had never completed such a number in a day. One man said, "We're sure the Lord must be pleased with the way you conserve the funds He provides."

For the first several years Audrey served as the makeup artist for the shoots. Today, a local hair stylist, Frankie Mikell, graciously offered to close her shop for the three or four days of taping and was an encouragement.

Recently the parade of provision was joined by Jane Crawford, daughter of board member Herb Simmons, and his wife, Norma. From Greenville, South Carolina, Jane teaches corrective makeup techniques to those who have undergone plastic surgery or who have other disfigurements. What a blessing it is to see the second generation in His service!

Another encouragement comes from Ellen Miller. She shops and selects my wardrobe for the 175 telecasts. It is a gargantuan task to coordinate ties, shirts, and other apparel for the shoots and to number each outfit.

The board members were kind enough to leave their work and come help us on our first four or five shoots. We could not have done it without them. Herb Simmons, a master craftsman, made the sets with the help of Dr. Grady McElmurray, a veterinarian, and Truitt Lively, a lawyer. What fun we had. On the first shoot when I didn't have enough clothes to make the changes, Norma Simmons went to see all the men in Metter who wore my size and borrowed their wardrobes. Jimmy Page, owner of WMAC, wore the same size trousers, shirts, and coats as I did. She took all of his clothes. Poor fellow! He had to come to our house to get enough clothes to dress for work.

Our beautiful Norwegian elkhound, Gea—named for Guido Evangelistic Association—enjoys being on camera with me. She went to obedience school in Atlanta and was brought up by expert instructor Ken Miller in his plane. She performs very well for the staff and for the many visitors who come to tour the gardens and studio. When I give the commands to heel, halt, or sit, she obeys flawlessly. I thought it would be a good idea to use her for a telecast lesson on obedience. The cameras were rolling, and I commanded, "Gea, sit." She sat. Then I said, "Gea, heel," and she walked obediently with me. But then she saw a butterfly, and away she ran to chase the beautiful butterfly. I immediately ad-libbed, "How like many of us Christians. The Lord says 'Follow Me' and we follow until we see a butterfly—a pleasure, a person, a position—and away we run instead of remaining with the Lord."

One day Gea made a most unusual impression on a one-armed man who came to the studio for help. Gea usually sits by my side, but this time she crawled under the coffee table and stayed between us. All the time he talked, Gea growled softly. The man said, "I'm demon possessed. I need help, and I believe you can help me. That's why I've driven all this distance." He went on, "One day in my room in Atlanta the demons told me to cut off my arm. I cried that I wouldn't, but from all around the room I heard voices crying, 'Cut it off! Cut it off!' I picked up my hacksaw and I cut it off. Another day they told me I wasn't fit to live.

I admitted it. Then they ordered me to shoot myself. I refused. But they kept insisting, so I picked up my pistol and shot myself twice." Gea kept on growling softly.

He continued, "I visited my father, who's famous, and spent the night in the guest room. During the night the demons told me to kill my father. I refused. They insisted. I took my pistol and quietly slipped into my father's room to shoot him. He woke up. I was arrested, and rightly so.

"I've had all kinds of cures and treatments, but I am no better. Here are papers that show I'm not lying. Oh, please help me."

My heart was deeply stirred, and I read to him the story of the Lord casting out demons, and said, "Let's kneel."

"No," he said.

So I knelt, and I prayed with all my heart, "Here's a man, dear Lord, whom Thou dost love, and for whom Thou didst die. Lord Jesus, cast out the demon of drink, the demon of lust, the demon of self-destruction, and come into his heart. Lord Jesus, please come into his heart and save him right now."

Suddenly the man dropped to his knees and cried, "Yes, Jesus, come in and deliver me now!" Then he started to cry, saying, "He's done it. He's done it!" At that, Gea jumped up and started licking his tear-streaked face and loving him. "Look!" he exclaimed. "The grace of God is even in your dog!"

After Gea appeared with me on a telecast, a stranger came by the gardens. "You have a beautiful dog. What's her name?" When I told him, he went on, "You must love her very much. I can tell by the way she responds to you."

"We do," I admitted.

"Why?"

I told him, "I suppose it's because her mother rejected her when she was a puppy. She still has a scar on her nose where her mother bit her. That touched us to see that little wounded nose, and she won our hearts."

Michael directed his next question directly to the visitor. "Have you ever been rejected and scarred? If you have, I want to be the first to tell you that the Lord loves you so much and gave Himself for you. Heaven and happiness can be yours if you accept Him. You will, won't you?"

He didn't answer. The seeds are sown, and some fall on good ground. But some simply fall between the cracks of human reason, the crevices of closed minds and the commercialization of living in this world. Mark 4:19 puts it this way: "And the cares of this world, the deceitfulness of riches, and the desires for other things entering in choke the word, and it becomes unfruitful."

Gea still costars in the programs now and then, sitting at my feet or fetching her favorite food, a green pepper from the vegetable garden. She's my version of Lassie.

Jeff Aaron, *Herald* staff writer from Statesboro, Georgia, captured his version of the Guidos' feat of completing six months of filming in six days. He writes:

Dressed in a dark-colored sweater with black shoes highly buffed, Michael Guido smiles and walks underneath a garden trellis. He sits down and peers into the camera lens.

And so another Guido production is under way.

The words: lights, camera, action are repeated incessantly for three days, twice a year, in the garden of Audrey and Michael Guido's evangelical association.

For the first time in over a year, on a Thursday afternoon, about twenty-five people arrived from Charlotte, N.C., to produce Guido's inspirational capsules entitled "A Seed from the Sower."

Well over two million dollars' worth of technical equipment arrived along with a director and producer to tape Guido sitting next to one of the garden's waterfalls, standing next to a piece of garden furniture or sitting with Gea, his Norwegian elkhound, spreading "the word of the Lord."

In previous years, after each "shooting," Guido has gone back to his book-filled study and begun researching for other stories to use on the next series of "messages," he said.

The parables Guido uses to augment his biblical

teachings are picked up through conversations with people he meets.

"Everyone I talk with, I'm always listening for an illustration or experience to use in the broadcast," Guido said as he lounged during a ten-minute dress change.

His messages are heard in every state in the union as well as in Europe and the Holy Land. They are broadcast on "numerous cablevision networks and Christian broadcasting systems like the PTL, Trinity and Liberty Broadcasting," he said.

Last Thursday, Friday and Saturday, with his wife acting as executive producer, he was involved in a rigorous schedule of filming 175 messages. Each day, he changed into about six different outfits.

Coloring is very important in taping, Mrs. Guido said. "In bright sunlight we wouldn't be able to use a light printed color. White doesn't work because it wears out and red 'bleeds' if Guido wears those colors," Mrs. Guido said.

Throughout the year, whenever the two buy clothes, they are always concentrating on the next shoot. Sometimes Mrs. Guido will buy something that Mr. Guido really doesn't like very much, "but he will wear it for the shoot whether he desires it or not," Mrs. Guido said and chuckled.

. . . Their approximately three-acre garden, which has received various awards from landscape architectural institutes, is cleaned every day. In fact, several days before the shooting, one of the gardeners goes through and sifts out dead plant leaves and blooms that are turning brown.

For the past twelve years since inaugurating his televised messages throughout the world, Guido has learned "to speak clearer and a little faster to get a little more into" each message.

In addition to filming more than the 175 messages twice a year, Guido writes four daily broadcasts and a weekly newspaper column.

Occasionally, Guido faces "writer's block," but he is soon back to writing after praying and asking "the Lord to give me things to go on," he said.

The 75-year-old evangelist works from five in the morning until around midnight. A spirited Guido said, "I wake up writing and I go to bed writing."

. . . For the past 45 years the Guidos have been sending their Christian messages to all parts of the globe.

ONE AFTERNOON WHILE I was digging in the garden, I noticed the same car driving by many times. Finally, when I had graduated to washing down the terrazzo and waving good night to the staff, the car slowed down. After all the cars in the parking lot were gone, the car drove in and parked. Out stepped a Catholic priest, a stranger to me. He immediately began sermonizing that surely it was beneath the dignity of a man of the cloth like the Sower to be cleaning off sidewalks and digging in the garden.

After we exchanged trivialities, the priest got down to why he had come: "I've been listening to your broadcast for many months now. I want assurance, the kind of assurance you have when you talk about God. And I want it now. I won't leave until I get it. However, you must know that I don't believe the Bible is the Word of God. I don't believe that Jesus was virgin-born, and I don't believe we are saved by grace. However, something is wrong in my life, and I feel it is right in yours. I want the real thing. Now, if you don't mind, I can stay all night until I get that assurance."

In just a few minutes, with the open Bible and a receptive mind, the priest found his assurance!

Another priest assisted us during the shoots in the early days of television. He would arrive around 5:30 A.M. and stay all day. He would say to me, "I know you need someone to pray with today, so let's pray." Other times he would do the most trivial tasks with joy. He would move heavy equipment for the crew, sweep walks, pull a weed, and encourage. On extremely hot days, when the temperature kept rising, he offered himself as a stand-in while cameras and lights were reset so that I could be out of the heat and resting. It was perfect because we resembled each other in complexion, and the preliminary work could be done with the priest while I got ready for the next set.

No protestant preacher ever stood in for me. How I love that priest! He had the ability to see what needed to be done. Without prompting, thanks, or recognition, he served the Lord with gladness.

As one evening approached, it was very warm, and Audrey had run out of ice. She was frantic! The stores were closed, and in just a few minutes she would feed the tired, hot, and hungry crew.

The dear, faithful priest overheard her concerns and promised, "I'll get it. Don't worry."

"Where?" Audrey asked. "Nothing is open."

"Don't ask me," he said. In just a few minutes he was back with all the ice needed. And his smile could have melted the ice!

Our gardens have won awards thanks to the careful planning of Roger Davis, a landscape architect from Augusta. He designed the videotaping garden in the early days of the concept. The McCorkles have continued over the years to donate material and their acumen for its beautification. In 1990 Skeeter McCorkle, C. S.'s grandson, will join the board of directors.

One day while we were taping fifty telecasts in the gardens, a mockingbird followed the crew around, singing all through the programs. The mockingbird has a song of its own but seldom uses it. Instead, it mimics the birds near it. Be it a pleasant, plaintive, or raucous song, it repeats whatever it hears.

Creating a beautiful garden in the Christian's life takes hard work and the patience of consistent work. Too many people are like mockingbirds. Whatever they hear, good or bad, they repeat. They do not have a testimony because they do not think on the Lord's teaching or their transformation.

In Psalms David exclaimed, in today's idiom, "Has the Lord

redeemed you? If He has, speak out. Tell others He has saved you."

Remember, God is not mocked. "Whatsoever a man soweth that shall he also reap."

Recently a board member came to visit. Looking into the garden from the study, he asked, "Who put that statue in your garden?"

"That's not a statue," I said. "That's a hired hand."

Right then I noted a minute message. Christians should be industrious, not idle; cultivated, not careless. A tree is known by its fruit, and a person is known by his work.

A man considering a new house bought it sight unseen. When he was asked if that wasn't very risky, he replied, "No. I know the builder. He builds his Christianity in with the bricks." Like that builder we try to tend our gardens with our Christianity.

Workers for the Lord are challenged to be "workmen that need not be ashamed . . . ones who work the works of our Father while it is day . . . who work for the night is coming." We are like God's art placed in the vast garden of the world for His glory and joy and the good of others.

A young artist painted a surrealistic picture of Jesus in the Garden of Gethsemane. It was a depiction that bothered many who viewed the work. It appeared to be without order or sequence until it was truly studied. The painter's garden had impressions of flowers and vegetables, with weeds amidst the magnificence.

One cannot help but wonder if this painting—a far cry from the paintings that hang in churches and bookstores of the same scene—doesn't depict a message that we sometimes miss. Jesus came into the world to save sinners, right where they are, within the confusion and contradiction of beauty and necessity, sin and righteousness.

The lovely setting of Guido Gardens and the impeccable care for each detail are tools to call people to repentance. The gardens are a background and backdrop for Michael's message that reaches young and old, rich and poor, in whatever state of mind and no matter what the circumstance. The gardens have one purpose—though the views may vary—to be a setting for the Master Gardener's "glory and joy."

The prayer chapel is an integral part of the gardens. Open twenty-four hours a day, it is architecturally pure for the location.

THE STAFF AND Audrey and I had prayed for a prayer chapel to grace the gardens for many years before God's answer was set in motion through the conversion of a station engineer in Savannah. Don Bigbie called our offices one morning, under conviction from what he had heard on the telecast. He had been unable to eat or sleep and had turned down an invitation to a New Year's Eve party.

He told me he had enjoyed the telecast very much. Then he began to cry and asked how to be saved.

Referring him to Revelation 3:20, I quoted the verse, "Behold, I stand at the door and knock. If anyone hears My voice and opens the door, I will come in to him, and dine with him, and he with Me." Then I mentioned other pertinent passages of Scripture. Minutes later, the young caller poured out his heart to God and acknowledged Jesus Christ as his Savior.

When Bigbie showed up at our offices, he asked, "Do you have a place for an engineer?"

I told him we did, but I cautioned him that we could not pay what he had been making at the station. "No matter," he said. "I would like to work for you and serve the Lord at the same time." He worked for the association for two years until his father started Savannah Communications and needed him in the new organization.

While Don Bigbie worked with us, he would share with his father the way God was working in our midst. His father became so interested that he would display Sower booklets at his communications business. During that time, the senior Bigbie felt an increasing burden for a prayer chapel at the Sower headquarters.

We continued to pray for a chapel of prayer and refuge for passersby or visitors to our work. The answer that unfolded was one in which we were "sorrowful yet rejoicing."

Bill Stillwell and his dear wife, Evie, were visiting. We looked out of the dining room window through pouring rain and saw a woman praying in the garden. With great sensitivity Evie said, "Oh, I hate to see her getting so wet while she is praying. Why don't you ask her to come into the studio?"

I hurried out and asked her to come inside. Her response was quiet but confident. "No. I want to be alone in God's presence here. My husband, Paul, is undergoing dialysis treatment at the hospital, and he needs my prayers very, very much. Just let me pray here in the rain."

When I related the conversation, Evie's caring response was, "What you need is a prayer chapel." I reminded her that for some time we had been praying for just that—the request was on our prayer board. Misty-eyed, she said, "Now I know why the Lord brought us to Metter. He wants me to give you the money for the prayer chapel. Have Jim Buckley design it, and I'll donate the funds you need."

The Bigbies provided the much-needed public address system, which plays music twenty-four hours a day. Evie and her husband returned for the ground breaking ceremonies, but she was called home to heaven before it was built. Bill took up his wife's promise and financed the chapel in her memory.

A short time before her death, Evie, knowing the terminal nature of her illness, confided that the Lord had brought her to Metter for "such a time as this." The chapel's possibility brought her joy. There was a neighbor who helped her, ministered to her, and was especially caring in Evie's final days. One day Evie told Bill, "If anything happens to me, I'd be very happy if you married Barbara. She's been wonderful to me."

After Evie graduated to heaven, Barbara and Bill became good friends, then fell in love. When he asked her where she wanted to be married, Barbara quickly answered, "The chapel in the pines with the Guidos." Theirs was a tender ceremony of solemnity and certainty. I knew God was pleased with the Stillwells' generous hearts. Thousands have since met God in a unique and individual way in that chapel. Many leave with a tune resonating from the choir loft of their hearts:

> I come to the garden alone,
> While the dew is still on the roses,

And the voice I hear,
Falling on my ear,
The Son of God discloses.
And He walks with me, and He talks with me,
And He tells me I am His own;
And the joy we share as we tarry there,
None other has ever known.

Austen Miles

Bill and Barbara Stillwell are faithful, loving board members who treasure the prayer chapel in their own meaningful way.

Bill provides new Buicks each year for the Guido Evangelistic Association. The license plates read "SOWER" and "SOWER II." Truckers have honked and motioned us over to the shoulder of the road to share life-changing experiences. On occasion, motorists follow us, hoping we will park soon, as if to say, "You helped me. You gave me just the word I needed." "Your program brought hope to a dope-addicted kid."

On and on the story of God's grace continues, as does the generosity of committed individuals like the Stillwells. Not everyone, however, accepts the program as strictly genuine.

ONE EVENING A young man came to the studio after everyone else had left. After I greeted him, he said, "I'm a student from Georgia Southern College. Some of us there listen to your broadcasts, watch your telecasts, and read your column. We wonder if you're a phony or for real."

I smiled and invited the young man into the offices.

"Wow!" he exclaimed, impressed by the furnishings and the surroundings. "What a nice-looking place. Where do you get the loot? You never ask for it."

"You're right. We don't ask people for money. We pray."

"Baloney," came the frank response. Smiling, I just continued walking down the hallway. When we came to a display with photographs of several items on the wall, the student wanted to know what it was.

"That's our prayer board," I explained. "Whenever we have a need, we put a picture of the item on this board, and every time we pass it we pray for the items."

Glancing at the board, the young man commented, "I see you're praying for several items. Do you think you'll get them?"

"No."

"See! Just as I thought. You're a phony!"

"You asked me if I *thought* we would get it. The answer is no, I don't think we'll get it; I *know* we will."

"Baloney," came the familiar response. We walked on down the hall and into my private office where the phone was ringing. I excused myself to take the call while the student sat back and waited.

Stating that he had just heard the broadcast and the message had blessed his heart, Truitt Lively was calling to see what needs the ministry had right then. He offered to pay for a tabletop folding machine, one of the items displayed on the prayer board. I beckoned the student over to the phone and asked Truitt to repeat his offer. As I held the receiver up to the young man's ear, Truitt repeated the conversation, "Buy it," he said again.

Leaping to his feet, the young man shouted, "I have seen a real-live answer to prayer!"

For the next few days, he dropped by to see if we'd had any further answers to prayer. His faith grew each time he visited, and before a week had passed, he trusted Christ as his Savior.

Larger audiences, as well, respond to the Sower's message. When they took visiting friends for a seafood dinner at a favorite Savannah restaurant, the hostess said to Michael, "The mixologist would like to see you at the bar."

He walked over to the bar, where a young woman greeted him. "I watch you every morning on WJCL-TV, and I hear you on WJCL-FM, but today is Saturday and you're not on radio or television. I was just talking with some of my customers, and they miss your programs today as much as I do. We wondered if you might be willing to share one of your television spots right here at the bar."

"I'd be honored," a surprised Michael replied. As he brought a brief message from the Word amidst the unusual surroundings, several listeners shed tears. These folks were reassured that Michael's message was genuine.

"Please pray for us," the mixologist said after Michael had finished.

INTERRUPTIONS LIKE THAT don't bother us. We look at them as God's opportunities—often they're opportunities to miss dinner, lose sleep, or work longer hours.

Audrey and I still like to think about the time when we faced our first video taping session, with 150 programs scheduled for production. We needed ten thousand dollars to proceed. With three weeks to go and the money still lacking, concerned board members suggested a loan, but I felt that was not the thing to do. God had never failed us yet.

Two weeks before the taping, a farmer, Sid Morgan of Sylvania, Georgia, invited us to join his family for Sunday dinner.

"How are things going?" Sid asked.

"Great!" I exclaimed.

"I mean financially."

"Terrible," I confessed, still smiling.

"Why? Just exactly what do you need?"

Again I smiled. "Just exactly ten thousand dollars," I said. Then I explained briefly about a taping session. With that, we changed the subject and enjoyed a delightful dinner together. Nothing more was said about our financial need.

A check for ten thousand dollars from the Morgans arrived in the next day's mail. We rejoiced and gave thanks to God, but as we discussed the gift, we became disturbed and called the Morgans. "Sid, we received your letter and we're most grateful, but you can't afford to give us the money. You have a son in medical school and two daughters in high school."

"I can't afford *not* to give it to you," Sid insisted. "Let me tell you why.

"My hired hand quit, and I couldn't take care of my hogs

alone so I had to sell them. I told Jean I'd deposit the proceeds the next day, but at dinner that evening I had to admit I'd failed to make the deposit. 'I'll do it tomorrow,' I promised her.

"While we were eating the next night, I had to admit again that I hadn't gotten around to the bank.

"Suddenly, Jean changed the subject. 'I can't get the Guidos off my mind,' she said to me. 'I can't either,' I told her. Then we decided to ask you for Sunday dinner and ask about your needs. We agreed that if you said a hundred dollars or a thousand dollars, we wouldn't give you anything, but if you said 'exactly ten thousand dollars,' we would give it. So now you know how it happened and why we *had* to give you the money."

"Thank you, Sid, and please thank Jean for us," I said. You really *can't* beat the Lord, can you?

Is the upkeep of the garden worth it? Does it pay to keep the beauty ever-ready for the next series of Sower programs? The answer has never been in question for the Guidos. They know the worth of a soul is immeasurable.

A couple from Tennessee watched the seeds come alive in their hearts through the programming. They longed to visit the gardens and see the locale of the productions. At last they arrived, elated, excited, and overwhelmed. They were living examples of the many people who trusted God after the Sower explained that God is never out of reach. Their prayer expresses it all:

Thank You, God, for this place. It holds untold secrets like ours. Secrets too personal to share, too deep to be understood. Thank You, God, for meeting us in our hour of need. For accepting us with our warts and wrinkles and wrongdoing. Thank You, God, that you ask for no credentials, for we have none, save the Jesus we asked into our hearts. Thank You, God—a lot!"

Only eternity will tell of those who have come to this garden—in person, by electronics, or through a booklet.

What is important is not how many. *The Lord never deals in masses, but individuals.* One woman at the well, one blind man at a pool, one fisherman on the shore of a lake. What is important to the Guidos is that they came to the Savior.

CHAPTER 12

Tho' the
Loss
Sustained

Rejoice evermore!
1 Thessalonians 5:16, KJV

Ask most Christians what the shortest verse in the Bible is and invariably they will come up with "Jesus wept." The Guidos would share together, "Rejoice evermore!"

And rejoice evermore they do. Any day and every day. With them, joy is an inside job, and nothing will rob that blessing. They rejoice in hope because they have a spontaneous song, and God requires us all to offer to Him the sacrifice of continual praise.

Praise God from whom all blessings flow! Relating those blessings in the form of changed and encouraged lives is as natural for the Guidos as eating or sleeping.

You have seen that there has been pain. And there is the ongoing pain for those who do not receive the message of Christ and ignore the precious invitation of "Whosoever will may come." The Sower and his lady grieve in their spirits at apathy and spoiled seed. But, grief does not hamper the sowing nor shut out their joy.

The late Norman Harrison related a story about being fascinated by a stream running through his father's pasture when he was young. Prone upon the bank of a quiet pool, he watched the bubbling up of crystal-clear water in numerous springs. As he grew in faith he recognized how much more inexhaustible than that fountainhead is the supply of God's joy, which the Lord would fain open as a bubbling-up fountain in the heart that believes and trusts Him. If the supply never fails, then why should the flow ever cease? Joy must overflow and touch those we meet to earn a hearing for the God we love and serve.

A bird hunter bought an expensive parrot and shipped it to his wife. When it arrived, she killed it, dressed it, and baked it. That evening the husband called to check on his bird. "Do you like it?" he asked.

"I can't tell yet," she answered, "it's baking in the oven now."

"In the oven?" he exploded. "That parrot spoke seven languages."

His wife replied, "Then why didn't he say something?"

Many people who are supposed to share the joy are fluent in many languages but vocal in none. Why don't we say something? Something that will change a life, with God's help. That is a question to be considered.

Our lives possess "designer genes" that are meant to perpetuate the fullness of joy, even though there may be a personal toll or felt loss.

Right when the Guidos needed additional land, an acre and a half across the street from the studio came on the market. They knew it would be a delightful location for a natural garden or a place to build a home for future personnel. Surveying the situation, they faced the fact that finances were low. As the song says, "our spirit often grieves," not from the lack of provision but from the knowledge of what more could be accomplished with greater provision.

Around Audrey's sixtieth birthday, some friends who owned a toy shop started a doll collection for her. Through the years they have pleased her with wonderful dolls, including the original boy and girl Cabbage Patch dolls. All the dolls were meaningful, registered, and expensive. However, the Cabbage Patch originals, with the added value of a personal autograph by the maker, were truly a collector's dream.

On Christmas Eve of 1982 a neighbor, Bill DeLoach, drove up in front of the offices. He came in with a deed to the acreage across the street in his hand. In exchange for the deed, he wanted the Cabbage Patch dolls as a gift for his wife, who was also a collector of fine dolls.

It was a difficult decision. The rare collection had been a joy to Audrey. She enjoyed sharing it with special friends and visitors, and it was something that was her own. She felt she should contact the dear ones who had provided the valuable dolls in the collection. Their wisdom would help her decision.

She called the Johnsons for permission to trade for the property which would then belong to the Guido Evangelistic Association. They were amenable. Audrey was temporarily disheartened, but wise. She gave the dolls. Giving is her nature, and she knew her loss was gain for the ministry. Hadn't our Lord said that the things we count gain, He often counts loss? Her priorities have never been in question when it comes to giving . . . not until it hurts but until it feels good!

"Loss sustained" also applies to the senior citizens and elderly who call the Sower for encouragement and hope. Their losses are recounted in feeling abandoned by family, lack of self-worth, and loss of mobility. They grieve over the phone about grandchildren on drugs, personal illness, disability, and lack of desire to live.

More than one senior relates the feeling of being cast on a junk heap of society. The emphasis today is on youth. People spend less time with grandparents or older adults—even parents—than they have at any other time in history.

Many men feel useless. Their talents and skill, accumulated over a lifetime, are no longer marketable. In an era when the population is getting older, this is a paradox. In 1820 about half of the country were under sixteen. In 1986 half were under thirty-one. It is predicted that by 2010, half will be under the age of forty. As the proliferation of nursing homes and care facilities attests, people are living longer.

The paradox is factored in because great talent is being ignored, and the country and church are missing valuable assets. Michael encourages these people. He reminds them that if a sparrow falls, God sees it, so how much more He sees each one as a cherished individual.

Others call to discuss the fragile moments and their fear in many of life's circumstances. Such was a caller who tried to ring immediately after Hurricane Hugo.

The home he shared with his wife was on the outskirts of the devastation. Their neighbor's trailer was upside down. Their own house was leveled. All their pictorial memories of yesterday were destroyed. Food and water were in short supply. The telephone lines were down.

During the days of wishing he could contact his unknown television friend, a revelation crossed this man's heart. He wrote,

> I was in need of talking to Mr. Guido. Getting his sympathy, knowing he would listen to me, console and give me words from my God. But the lines remained down. The communication was cut. It was then I remembered a little Sower booklet and its message. It talked about a kid who wanted a pony more than anything in the world. He started asking God to send him a pony. Then he carefully tied a rope to the post at the foot of his bed. The father came in and asked about the rope. The reply of childlike faith came, "That's the rope to tie the pony to my bed when it comes."

The Hurricane Hugo survivor went on to share that he did not have to talk to the Sower. He could talk with the Sower's Source. He called on God. There were no downed lines, no busy signal. God's power was there all the time. To celebrate the revelation, the gentleman found a piece of rope, cut it to the desired size, and forced it through one of his larger buttonholes. For many weeks of cleanup, the rope was a symbol of the One who held heaven's end! How he rejoiced.

A lady in her eighties contacted the Sower. She lived as an isolate in crowded conditions with an alcoholic son, his girlfriends, and scattered others who came and left. In utter pain and anguish, with her Social Security check going directly to the irresponsible son, she was immobilized. At times she feared for her life.

The only brightness of the day shone when those "seeds" came through the poorly tuned television and into her heart in the lowest of low-cost housing. "I wonder if the man in Metter knows how God's rays temporarily displace our darkness," she wondered.

Another caller had Parkinson's disease. With no one to transport her to a free clinic and no money for medication, she had given up hope. Her alienation was invaded by a tattered little booklet she picked up on a bus. It was called *Seeds from the Sower*. It brought life again—and victory—to an aging victim.

Michael and Audrey's great gift of encouragement lifts people of all ages. And it restores their self-worth and spiritual dignity, even amidst poverty and sadness. They care enormously and intimately. And that care comes through the pages of the booklets, beautifully prepared and printed.

They encourage those in later life, often through the story of Caleb in the Bible. A man who was meaningful to the purposes of God in *all* seasons of his life. Often called the most fearless in his old age, he wrote, "I wholly followed the Lord" (Josh. 14:8). His life proved there were no conditions, no reservations, no exemptions.

LONELINESS IS AN EQUAL OPPORTUNITY DESTROYER

WITHOUT THE COMFORT and compassion of the Lord, scores of readers, callers, and viewers would be in direr straits.

Possibly a reader of this book is discouraged just now and feels troubled and time-worn, like many senior adults. Possibly one is handicapped and feels dismayed. Insecurities and handicaps do not have to hinder you. Look what Beethoven did despite his deafness—he wrote music. Thomas Edison, deaf in one ear, was the father of audio. Braille acted on blindness and gave hand-sight to Braille readers.

Age does not have to abuse you. George Bernard Shaw wrote a play when he was ninety-three, and Grandma Moses was still painting pictures at one hundred. George Burns says if the next ninety-five are as good as the past ones, he is in for one big time!

"My biggest problem," said a dog trainer for the blind, "is to lift the eye level of the dog to the eye level of a person, so the dog can see his obstructions."

We need to raise our eye level too. We look at people and we see their mistakes. But humans make miserable models. We look at our circumstances and conditions and become crestfallen. We become selfish and our major cry is "What have you done for me lately?" when we have done little for ourselves.

We need to keep our eyes on Jesus. Then when He becomes Savior, He will become your Source, Resource, and Goal. We will conquer, not be conquered by, the visible. Jesus wants to be our invisible means of support.

Michael writes for the Dial-A-Prayer program each day, preparing a new prayer to be presented by phone. Most are simple petitions like this one:

> Heavenly Father, cleanse me from all my sins and
>   keep me clean this day.
> Inspire me to meditate on Thy Word and to think
>   about ways to follow Thee more closely.
> Constrain me to live in purity, to act in love, to
>   speak in truth, and to witness for Thee in
>   power.
> Help me all through this day to be prayerful,
>   joyful, and thankful. Through Christ, Amen.

If staff members delay placing the new taped prayer on the machine, they usually hear about it from concerned callers. Once a surprised caller realized she had dialed a wrong number. Trying to call a local restaurant, she heard instead this Dial-A-Prayer:

> Heavenly Father, I present my body to
>   Thee as a living sacrifice.
> Give me Thy love for my heart, Thy
>   wisdom for my mind, and Thy skill for
>   my hands.
> Make me equal to every experience, ready
>   for every responsibility, and adequate for
>   every task. Help me to serve Thee
>   enthusiastically.
> So bring me to the end of this day with
>   nothing left undone and with nothing to
>   be ashamed of. In the name of Jesus,
>   Amen.

She called the Association offices a short time later. "I wanted food for my body, but the Lord knew I needed food for my soul. Thanks very much for your prayer."

Most of the Sower publications tell about Dial-A-Prayer and give the phone number, so the outreach is vast. Some callers memorize the prayer while others make it a vital part of their daily devotions.

One of the other writing projects that demand Michael's time and attention, *Seeds from the Sower,* is a small daily devotional booklet for one month at a time. It typifies the Guido style:

THAT BOY'S ANNOYING ME
READ 1 PETER 5:7

A GIRL CRIED, "That boy's annoying me!"

"Dear," replied her mother, "he's not even looking at you."

"I know," she admitted. "That's why he's annoying me."

But the Lord's looking at you. The Living Bible says, "He is always thinking about you and watching everything that concerns you."

I know there are many who say with the psalmist, "There is no one who takes notice of me; no one cares for me." But they're wrong.

The Lord takes notice of you. He has even numbered the hairs of your head. His eyes are upon you, His ears are open to you, and His arms are underneath you.

Why don't you put your trust in this faithful Friend who loves you?

When a woman stopped at the Tulare Inn in Tulare, California, a copy of the tract *This Is Important* lay on a dresser in her room. That twelve-page booklet, printed in both English and Spanish, has headings that reveal the nature of the message: "The Lord Loves You"; "You Need To Be Saved"; "You Cannot Save Yourself"; "Jesus Can Save You"; "Jesus Can Keep You"; "Here's When You Should Be Saved"; "Here's How You Can Be Saved"; "My Decision"; and "Now That You Are Saved."

Like scores of other motels across the country, the inn keeps every room supplied with the tracts and daily devotional booklets. Strengthened by the message of *This Is Important*, the Tulare guest felt led to take the tract along with her as she visited her dying father, an agnostic. Maybe her father would find in it the truth that she had been unable to convey.

Later, at her father's bedside, the woman enjoyed a pleasant time of conversation with him. When he fell asleep, she left the leaflet on the nightstand beside his bed and left. Returning the next morning, she thought he looked different. "Thank you for leaving that little booklet with me," he said. "I read it, and I want you to know that before the evening was over I trusted Christ as my Savior."

Buoyed by such reports, staff members redouble their efforts to distribute their literature.

Similar reports refer to another ministry of the Sower, one that began because of an enterprising newspaper editor. "Will you write a regular newspaper column for us?" asked the editor of the Metter *News and Advertiser*. Thus began a newspaper column that now has nationwide circulation. The association furnishes camera-ready copy for the weekly column.

Some of the more than fifteen hundred newspapers that carry the column express their appreciation. Charles M. Williamson, editor and publisher of *The Darien News* in Darien, Georgia, wrote: "This is the best article we are privileged to publish." Editor Jimmy Anderson of the *Georgia State Prison News*, Reidsville, echoed that view.

The range of subject matter is wide. Here is a typical day's selection:

> One day I looked out of our windows and wondered, "Why don't our neighbors wash their dirty windows?"
>
> But when I washed our windows, I saw that their windows were clean.
>
> Now when I am tempted to criticize others, I ask, "Am I looking through my dirty windows?"
>
> Our Lord said, "Do not judge, or you too will be judged." Criticism is a bludgeon and a boomerang.
>
> If we judge, we will be judged. By whom? Our Father in heaven and our fellows on earth.
>
> So only the faultless has a right to look for faults in others. We have enough to correct in our lives without seeking to correct the lives of others.
>
> Our Lord said, "Why do you look at the speck of sawdust in your brother's eye and pay no attention to the plank in your own eye?"
>
> It is only as the Spirit of Christ dominates us that the spirit of criticism will depart from us.

Tapes, too, make their impact on lives. Gerald H. Achenbach, founder of the large Piggly-Wiggly grocery chain, took the Sower's tapes on the Book of Revelation with him on a ten-day vacation trip to Jamaica. He spent the afternoons listening to them. "When I came home, I felt like an authority on the book. Michael communicates the Word of God in a way you can understand."

Every Christmas, Achenbach sends sets of the tapes as gifts to business leaders in Vidalia, Georgia, where he has retired to Rocky Creek Farm. "I like people who give 120 percent of their time, energy, and talent. The Guidos do that."

They put that same effort into their monthly publication, *Sowing and Reaping*, the association's house organ, a six-page accordion-fold leaflet containing poems, anecdotes, excerpts from books and articles, promotional bits, and news items, both religious and secular. As in most of their literature, snatches of humor occasionally appear.

Longer booklets, up to sixteen pages, are a part of the monthly mailing and cover a variety of topics. Many publications are requested in quantity. The power of the written word is still much mightier than the sword.

The people who have sustained loss through fractured families, extensive conflict, suicide, and physical failures cannot be counted. Nor can the message that comes to them through the Sower ministries. As with Johnny Appleseed—who knows the multiplication of one seed?

God has promised, He will watch over His word to perform it. No wonder Michael and Audrey "rejoice evermore."

CHAPTER 13

WE SHALL COME REJOICING, BRINGING IN THE SHEAVES

Then He said to His disciples, "The harvest truly is plentiful, but the laborers are few. Therefore pray the Lord of the harvest to send out laborers into His harvest."

Matthew 9:37–38

Earlier chapters in this book were titled, "We Shall Come Rejoicing" and "Bringing in the Sheaves." Why repeat the captions again—this time in combination?

The Guidos, after their tragic accident, made the determination to do the work of two couples rather than one. Through the years this doubling of their efforts for God's kingdom has become natural. They are acutely aware of what prompted the Apostle Paul to write, "*Re*joice in the Lord always. Again I will say, *rejoice*" (Phil. 4:4).

Together they have maintained their conscious commitment to increase their joyful sowing consistently, working in the energy of the Spirit of God, with rejoicing. They still seek to be controlled not by "outward" circumstances but by "inward" sources. For they "repeatedly" come rejoicing, bringing in the sheaves.

Paul, the apostle, knew the basis of his joy. It was never easy to rejoice in adversities like jail terms, beatings, shipwrecks, or litigation. Yet he redoubled his efforts to remain joyful. One does not rejoice in the difficulties, but rejoices *in the Lord*, the Bible teaches. That is the key: rejoicing in the sovereignty of Almighty God. Then the difficulty becomes the means for rejoicing, the mountain becomes the way, and the obstacles become the vehicle.

Michael and Audrey know that "bringing in the sheaves" is a command of God, not just His casual recommendation. Each believer is invited to become an ordained soul winner. How? By divine appointment. For each person of faith is commanded, commended, commissioned, and compelled to share the life-changing message of Jesus. It is the gospel (good news) of eternal life!

When Michael came to the Lord Jesus, his feeling was similar to that of an older lady who received a telegram one day, informing her that she had just inherited a thousand dollars. She dropped her knitting and ran to the phone shouting, "Hello, operator. Get me anybody!"

In realizing Christ died for his sins, saved his soul, and had a plan for his life, Michael Guido wanted to tell everyone—everywhere.

Today he relates that

HALF THE THRILL of getting the news that "anyone who calls upon the name of the Lord will be saved" comes from telling others about Him after you are saved. Want a thrill? Call on the Lord; and then invite others to call on Him. It's more than a duty to witness for our Lord; it's a delight to become a winsome witness and be obediently His to command, wherever He leads.

Commanded?

Let the redeemed of the LORD say so (Ps. 107:2).

Commended?

> Those who are wise shall shine
> Like the brightness of the firmament
> And those who turn many to righteousness
> Like the stars forever and ever (Dan. 12:3).

Commissioned?

> Therefore we are ambassadors for Christ . . .
> (2 Cor. 5:30).

Compelled?

> Other sheep I have which are not of this fold;
> them also I must bring . . . (John 10:16).

Why do some people achieve more than others? Educators and philosophers have long argued the question. Why do some develop their talents and abilities to a greater degree than others? With all things being equal, the answer must come from the "within." Taking what has been given by God, developing it for His glory, and taking Him at His word—these are resources to be used, not abused, and then returned to Him.

Phillips Brooks wrote that "God can take a man's nothingness and when he links it to God's almightiness, things happen. Yea, when man is willing to study God's word, God's plan, and outwork God's purpose, greater will be the expansiveness of service. Earthly and heavenly rewards will follow and compound."

Because that is the Guido pattern, those close to them in the work have discernibly the same outlook. Staff members, trained by Audrey, go the extra mile and give their full measure of devotion to their work. Of the ten ministry support staff, two work in the gardens; eight, in the studio.

Efficiency experts relate that with the business

transacted, the programs made, and all the other major tasks accomplished, they produce as much as a staff of *twenty-five!* The extraordinary effort at the Guido marketplace overwhelms visitors. Following the example of their bosses, the staff graciously define their contribution as "our reasonable service."

The fruitfulness of the seeds of ministry in human hearts motivates the association's board of directors. These strong, caring, and successful business people find profound challenges in the unselfishness of the founders and the dedication of the Lewis Street workers. One board member observed, "The Chamber of Commerce boasts that 'Things Are Better In Metter.' I'm convinced that's true on our grounds. The talent and efficiency are astounding. Michael could be a talk show host on any network, USA. Audrey has all the capabilities to run a multimillion-dollar corporate headquarters and make it more profitable with fewer people. However, we know Metter is not the cause. It is God who multiplies these herculean efforts in His own way. I'm blessed to be a part."

As the media ministries grew, Michael chose to be accountable to a board as well as his chief accountant and advisor—the Lord Jesus Christ.

The board membership is diverse, and the members' introduction to the ministry has been as varied as the areas of expertise they represent. They are official rejoicers as well as participants in this old-fashioned faith method of trusting God for everything.

They never solicit funds for the work. They join the friends of the ministry in keeping up with the well-worn prayer board. They freely give their time, their advice, and their money. Many times they have been moved to answer their own prayers!

FOR MANY YEARS we owned an automobile called Flattery— because it got us nowhere. It kept us strapped even without seat-belts. One mechanic even suggested we should "keep the oil and change the car!"

We had asked the Lord to make a way for us to buy a car. His answer was a pleasant surprise. Board member Bill Stillwell came from Illinois to visit the garden. Later he told me, "I told the Lord that when He gave us a Buick agency, you would never have to buy a car. He gave us the dealership in Downers Grove, and here is your new Electra. Every year when you reach ten thousand miles, I'll bring a new replacement." He continues this valuable service. Twice a year our loaners are sold across the United States.

Their meeting was not a coincidence. In April 1952 the Guidos had returned to Bill's church. For some months Bill and his wife had heard accolades of the Sower and his lady. They could not believe two people could be so talented. The young people remembered their messages and magic from the previous year and were excited about a return engagement.

The Stillwells and Guidos became instant friends. God brought the families together in a bond of love and unity.

Never seeking aggrandizement from the ministry or board, the Guidos are reluctant to accept praise or honors. Very few are hung in their offices, and none can be found in the home. However, the Stillwells' evaluation is valid. "Buick Bill" writes,

To be with the Guidos is like a breath of air from heaven. They live and breathe the love of Jesus, and to be near them is such a joy and blessing. To visit the gardens, the studio, and the home is just like stepping into hallowed ground because we know that everything—from each blade of grass to the most expensive building—has been given to be used to proclaim the gospel of our Lord Jesus. Each item, large or small, has been prayed for and received and dedicated for that purpose alone. The Guidos have been a very active influence on our total lives personally and in business, and we love them and rejoice in our part of the association. Three generations in my family have heart involvement. When one of my sons has a concern, he calls Michael—then prays!

Grady and Thera McElmurray would agree with all of the above! Grady is a veterinarian who retired early to have more time for service. Thera was touched by the Sower in 1941. Grady met him in 1969. Writes Grady,

When I think of the parable of the sower in Mark 4, I think of Michael and Audrey Guido. When I hear the birds singing, like on their television program, I think of Michael and Audrey. When I hear the song "Bringing in the Sheaves," I think of Michael and Audrey.

My wife is my closest and dearest friend. Michael was her childhood idol. This piqued my interest. Then after we attended a high school reunion in Metter, we went by to greet the man she had known during those years. I was impressed most of all by the sweet, loving way he said the name of Jesus. Not long afterward, I was asked to consider serving on the board of directors. I accepted. Through the years we have grown to love these people more each day. I think of them as brother and sister, father and mother, friends, pastors, counselors, clients, and fellow workers in the Lord's vineyard.

As clients, during the lives of their two dogs, we saw tender, compassionate hearts with animals. Doc, a big German shepherd with a deep bass voice, ruled the studio for years as he served as watchdog and companion for Audrey and Michael, especially for Audrey when Michael was on speaking assignments.

I knew Doc in his senior years. The dog had developed painful hip displasia. I performed surgery and prescribed medication over the years to give some relief. When the pain was too intense,

and the suffering too great, the decision was made
to let him go to sleep humanely. This is a task no
veterinarian likes to perform. Michael and Audrey
loved this companion and showed their grief.

Doc was succeeded by their Norwegian elkhound, a soft, thick-coated dog with a loose
tongue and a tail that responds like a happy met-
ronome. It is not surprising their hearts reach out
to "fur persons" as well as "all persons." All crea-
tures, great and small, occupy pieces of their
hearts.

We have watched them in most events of life.
Some of the most trying being the semiannual
television tapings. My recollections are vivid: hot
weather; times when everything goes wrong; enormous cost-per-second knowledge in these TV
shoots when the financial clock is ticking. Pressure. Pressure. Pressure. Michael keeps his cool
and is usually ready for a laugh in the middle of it
all. He constantly prays, committing it to the
Lord.

During this time, Audrey is behind the scenes
directing each move to ensure that equipment
functions promptly and efficiently and all personnel are doing the utmost to see that the show goes
on. This is TV taping at its most beautiful and its
most economical! Hours of reading the scripts
over and over, without varying a second, with
proper inflection and expression, show Michael as
the dedicated professional he is. Ready to praise
personnel who are trying to correct any problems
which may arise, both calmly perform. Michael,
in front of the camera, and Audrey, behind the
scenes, being sure all moves with dispatch—for
God's glory.

Michael enjoys life and demonstrates it in many
ways. He can write you a sermon with his multi-
tude of melodious, merry, meticulous words that

motivate you to meditate on the Lord Jesus Christ. But don't ask him to tighten a loose screw around the place. Call Audrey. She will organize the situation to peak efficiency and can understand and implement most technical manuals. She figures budgets to the penny and stretches a dollar so far that poor George Washington becomes five feet wide! She combines the bargaining ability of a street vendor with that of an astute, rich Wall Street broker.

These people complement each other and compel us, by their example, to rejoice more and sow seeds that will find good soil in people of all ages.

Children love the ministry. When introduced to Michael at our church, one of the youngsters affectionately referred to him as the "Tweety-bird Man." Our nephew, just a tot when he met Michael, said, "I knew you would be smiling from the way you sound on the radio! I'll never forget your story of Humpty Dumpty."

Michael remarks:

THERE IS A nursery rhyme

> Humpty Dumpty sat on a wall.
> Humpty Dumpty had a great fall.
> All the king's horses and all the king's men
> Couldn't put Humpty Dumpty together again.

Michael remarks, "Strange, isn't it? They called on the king's men and horses, but not on the king!"

In Clearwater, Florida, rather than staying in a hotel as was customary, Michael stayed in a guest house at the home of Herb and Norma Simmons, who were having a difficult time in their Christian lives. After spending time in the Word with the visiting evangelist, the couple

learned they did not have to endure a spiritual
breakdown. There was a spiritual breakthrough. People
who were church members had been dishonest. It was
Christians who had let them down. Christ never does.
Christ does not just *have* integrity; He *is* integrity.

Their times together were revealing and refreshing, and
for Herb and Norma, restoring. In 1975 Herb joined the
board of directors. Norma has added her beautiful design
touches to the offices. Both are treasured friends. In
chorus, while discussing their friends in Metter, the
Simmonses say, "What a team! Only in the record of
heaven will the great and mighty works from that tiny
place on the Georgia landscape be known."

The Simmonses are delighted that their children also
support the association, and their grandchildren love
Michael and Audrey. Three generations—proof positive
that "one generation shall praise Your works to another, /
And shall declare Your mighty acts" (Ps. 145:4).

Echoing a sentiment expressed by another board
couple, Wayne and Alene Denning agree that the Guidos
are like family, confidants, and the truest of friends.
Wayne and Alene met Michael and Audrey in Tulare,
California. The four often visited between meetings, and
their lasting impression is that the Guidos always promote
Christ. Not themselves. Not their organization. They
consistently lift the Lord Jesus Christ to His rightful
position of exaltation.

The Dennings found this special. They watched the
Guidos give out the gospel freely—in restaurants or
parking garages, and to all people they meet, they give
a Sower booklet. Another seed from the Sower! The
Dennings became firsthand observers of Michael's
statement of faith-finances: "We have something for the
people and do not want something from them. If we do
God's work in God's way, He will supply our needs."

This friendship spans thirty years. The Dennings
became board-associated in 1980 and are staunch
supporters for many reasons. One good reason comes in

the package of their seven-year-old boy. Leroy accepted the Lord when Michael was holding a revival in the Dennings' hometown. The ministry touched their own household with young Leroy's conversion.

Bread is the staff of life. Bonita and Joseph Hamstra met Michael when he held a revival in Pastor James Holbrook's church. They broke bread together in a restaurant one morning. To this day they are amazed that they were singled out of a congregation of three thousand to participate in this event. True to character, Michael was "sowing in the morning." The seeds fell on good ears, and Bonnie and Joe, as they are affectionately known, were eager listeners to Michael's story.

Joe says that from the beginning he was astounded at the incredible outreach of a ministry that made no specific solicitations. Today as board members Joe and Bonnie assist in many ways, such as providing Hamstra Hideaway, a two-unit guest facility built into the much-used warehouse.

The couple's foresight in providing these "prophet's chambers" has been appreciated by other board members, friends, relatives, and past associates of the Guidos. The guest books placed in each facility read like a spiritual "Who's Who," and the expressions of love for the host and hostess at times defy reality.

Coauthorship of this book brought me the pleasure of staying in this facility. My sister, Bonnie Jepson, and I were weekend residents at Hamstra Hideaway. We were grateful for board members who believed in quality and warm ambience. The dressers were dotted with Sower booklets, and wonderful sayings enhanced the tables. Most of all, the love of the Guidos was richly expressed. Our arrival was delayed. At one in the morning we were barely settled when Michael called to say that he and Audrey were bringing over, via the golf cart, freshly baked blueberry pie. That alone would have been more than expected, but frosted over the top of the bubbling berries was delicious ice cream!

In that thoughtful provision there was a graphic

expression of the Guidos. Nothing is too much when it comes to serving people. This superabundance represented not just care but intense care for very late and weary travelers. Through the weekend these evidences of thoughtfulness and kindness reached world-class proportions.

The Hamstras say that knowing they have met a need, fresh from their hearts of love to the Guidos and guests, brings them great joy. They often express their love in true designer ways.

Through mutual friends, Don and Lois Ann Coker of Turbeville, South Carolina, met the Guidos when they were holding meetings in that area. Coker felt a concern to reach his employees with the message of Christ. The idea germinated. He asked Michael to fly to his plant to talk with the staff and workers. Coker employed about three hundred to build modular condominiums.

Shedding his coat and tie, Michael loved sharing the Lord amidst the lathes and laborers, the draftsmen and designers. He felt he was indeed in the marketplace of life. For four years Michael flew monthly to the production plant. Coker relates:

> We had a survey conducted by a professor from Appalachian State University in Boone, North Carolina, to research employee attitudes toward the company. The professor advised us that a positive response of 40 percent would usually be considered excellent. He was astonished when presenting his findings several weeks later— positive response to the Guido sessions ran eighty-one percent.
>
> The Sower has a God-given ability to speak God's truth in love with equal ease and effectiveness to shop workers, migrant workers, educators, professionals, or heads of state.

In all this diversity unity of purpose binds the board together with the Guidos in prayer and mutuality.

Members, like members of the body of Christ, function by praying for wisdom and understanding, never losing sight of the goal—to win people to Christ.

Truitt Lively, a Houston lawyer who has been a member of the board for two decades, shares his enthusiasm. "The exciting thing to me is that from a small town in a beautiful part of Georgia so much is accomplished for the good of the world with such a small amount of money." Truitt has been a stalwart support, using his legal skills as tools and his large heart for souls. As a land developer, he knows dollar value. He is proud of the Guido Evangelistic Association and, as if making a court summation, says, "More gospel comes out of here for the dollar than anywhere else in the world."

He and his wife, Barbara, call the offices often to encourage their client/friends and offer love and prayers for the staff. They believe Michael is "the epitome of faith in his attitude, his productivity, his commitment to the Lord, and His work."

The Livelys participate joyfully in Metter events, and when the Welch Memorial Studio was dedicated some years ago, the whole family came for the celebration.

Traveling with Michael in the Holy Land, the attorney was impressed by his consistency, warmth, and personality in their two-week, face-to-face encounter. There Michael felt led to discuss Lively's vision for the television ministry featuring the one-minute messages now presented between soap operas, newscasts, advertisements, and late, late shows. A vision that was inspired by God.

The Livelys and other board members believe the Scripture that best describes Michael, Audrey, and their work is "But by the grace of God I am what I am, and His grace toward me was not in vain, but I labored more abundantly than they all; yet not I, but the grace of God which was with me" (1 Cor. 15:10).

The Puritans used to say that grace is the prelude to gratitude, which displays itself in graciousness. Obviously, that is the grace of God the Guidos evidence.

Yet the Guidos would say these evaluations are not needed. They work for God, and His "well done" is their highest desire. But the board wanted their say! Too often they have heard disbelievers say this ministry is not possible or plausible. It is too good to be true. Combining their hundreds of years of relationships with the Sower and Audrey, this board presents a respect and love uncommon in today's Christian circles.

When Corrie Ten Boom, the valiant Holocaust survivor, was complimented, she felt unworthy and tended to brush off the praise or turn aside. One day she stopped to ponder the encouraging words. She recounted her blessings and called them flowers. For each compliment that came, she added a stem to an imaginary bouquet. When her schedule was packed and the words of gratitude poured in, the flowers were abundant. At other times, scarce. Each night she collected the invisible blossoms and laid them at the feet of Jesus. Her gift may be best described by Theodulph of Orleans in the eighth century:

> All glory, laud and honor
> To Thee, Redeemer, King.
> To Whom the lips of children
> Made sweet hosannahs ring.
> The company of angels
> Are praising Thee on high,
> And mortal men and all things
> Created make reply.
> Thou didst accept their praises
> Accept the praise we bring,
> Who in all good delightest,
> Thou good and gracious King!

The bouquets the Guidos present to their Lord must be lavish.

Speaking of flowers, the newest board member will be D. E. "Skeeter" McCorkle, whose grandfather, C. S., has been a dear friend and provider of the Guido gardens' growth, greenery, and design for many years. Skeeter is third-generation in a family nursery business that in this decade will celebrate half a century.

Grandfather took Skeeter "walking, talking, and fishing" in his preschool years. But his greatest admiration for C. S. comes because of his "godly wisdom, his inward motivation, his way of making every day count for something important."

The senior McCorkle passed on to his grandson qualities that Skeeter will bring to the board. He is strong in accounting and loves working with people. His background in preparing soil, planting, watering, and harvesting has great eternal value.

Skeeter and his wife, Maria, are eager to work closely with the Guidos and board members.

When Skeeter joins this group on the association board, he too will sign an annual pledge and statement of faith indicating his desire to remain in that position.

At the upcoming board meeting, members will use their best persuasive powers to encourage Michael and Audrey to take a vacation. But the Guidos will decline. They are convinced this is not the time for a passport to vacation or retirement. They are too excited about every new day and the opportunity it brings. They faithfully claim, "As thy days, so shall thy strength be," recognizing the task at hand is sowing seeds and gathering fruit and flowers to put at the feet of Jesus. After all, that is their mandate and true imperative, making their theme song more than words and music. It is their life and lifestyle.

> We shall come rejoicing,
> Bringing in the sheaves.

PART FOUR

CHAPTER 14

THE SOWER AND HIS LADY

What we did not have . . . He provided.
What we did not know . . . He knew.
What was unforeseen . . . He foreordained.
What is certain . . . God is adequate.

The prayers of Michael and Audrey Guido have never been for personal gain or public acclaim. They have prayed only that they would be *adequate* for the entrusted task and that they would show unconditional love.

You have already read of some simple and dramatic answers to prayer. The heart of their prayers does not change, but today they have added the desire for more stations and greater exposure to plant more *Seeds from the Sower*. The knowledge that those seeds come to life through the screen of a television, the receiver of a radio, or the printed page is the driving motivation.

Together the Guidos have assimilated into their Christian walk the truth that faith and obedience are synonymous. As in intended love and marriage, "you can't have one without the other."

"Faith is 90 percent courage," says Michael. "The balance of faith is endurance and tenacity or what the Bible calls 'the substance of things hoped for and

the evidence of things not seen.' Faith includes belief
but *faith is action*."

Both are familiar with the meaning of grabbing hold of
a promise of God and grasping it tightly. They have never
found God's arms too short to reach out to them as
individuals or meet a ministry need. They believe that

> God is not a man, that He should lie,
> Nor a son of man, that He should repent;
> Has He said, and will He not do it?
> Or has He spoken, and will He not make
>   it good? (Num. 23:19).

They are also aware that just because He does not act
does not mean that He is incapable or inadequate. Much
to the contrary. C. S. Lewis said, "God answers prayers
in two ways. Yes! Or My grace is sufficient for thee."
That "sufficient grace" is a great stabilizer for the Guidos.
Therefore they exhibit a willingness to endure when the
promises are not visible, assured within that what God
wills, He does, and it will be good. Michael says:

AT TIMES IT'S difficult to separate our responsibility from God's
responsibility. D. L. Moody urged in those situations of life to
"work like it depends on you and trust like it depends upon
God." It is certain He will lead. God is the Boss, and it is important that His children understand that the Christian walk is a
journey, not just a destination. God's highway leads to heaven,
but the on-ramps, detours, and off-ramps, for the faithful, are of
His choosing.

Audrey and I share central dynamics. Irrevocable mandates.
They are prayer, the Word, profitability, accountability, and
great love and respect for people. We treasure our marriage and
handle it like a rare chalice of irreplaceable value.

Each gift that comes our way is precious. It may be a coin
wrapped in the corner of a worn-out handkerchief—given for
booklets. It may be some freshly picked fruit or vegetables from
a neighbor's garden. A special gift comes from Audrey's

mother—fresh fish caught in the lake on the outskirts of Metter before the dawn on a still morning. We find tear-stained notes or funds for a major piece of equipment in the prayer chapel. Each one is a blessing—and we are grateful before God. For life itself we thank God every day.

A passion for excellence accompanies their work's sole objective—the widest possible distribution of God's love. Critics say they give of themselves to an extreme. Few deny this. For when you first meet Michael and Audrey, you see two uniquely integrated, but separate, packages, tied together with one glorious ribbon of love. When the packages are unwrapped, you discover a touching celebration of what it means to be human! You will also observe two gracious people who appear too good to be real. They give 400-percent performance, with efficiency and encouragement to coworkers. Theirs is a united commitment to go the extra mile, stretching it to a miracle mile. These are people who work hard, and say, tongue in cheek, "We're saving our apathy for a failure!"

One gentleman who would like to have written a story about the Guidos said, "I would call the book *One Incredible Life and an Intelligent Wife* or, as I think about it, how about *The Sowing-Machine Man?*" Becoming more serious he wrote:

> I had been an archenemy to God. My life was a lurid picture, out of control morally, feeling immunized against help or recovery. I had sown innumerable seeds of liquid comfort (alcohol), compulsive behaviors, and irresponsibility. I was literally falling apart at the seams in body and soul. I perceived God as some noninsurable policy that might or might not pay off in time. The time came, in the form of the Sower's syndicated newspaper column. I wrote for more information and learned that God was not an abstract concept but a Person named Jesus Christ. That "sowing ma-

chine" outdid any the Singer Corporation could manufacture to mend my brokenness. I just want to keep thanking the Lord for life and life everlasting.

Michael and Audrey pour out such stories of God's work. Always kind, Michael ministers God's love, forgiveness, and hope in the intimate moments of counseling. He has a unique way of connecting people to the Father. One whose life was changed said, "His lucid and easy-to-read seeds combined with our caring sessions brought me to my knees and elevated me to the Savior. He knows how to show care to a careless world. He taught me to be an eraser of negative feelings after we negotiated, through the blood of the Lamb, with the Father. The trails of that ministry resemble the contrails of a great plane reaching for heaven."

Michael and Audrey have never kept track of fruit and are hard-pressed to present statistics of their own making. They don't file confidential conversations or store the thousands of letters that arrive each week. But they do respond in person and by letter to those who want more help. In person, by telephone, by letter, the needs compound. Michael and Audrey are caring catalysts,— even in the earliest moments of a new day.

AT 3:00 ONE morning I answered the doorbell to find a woman dressed in a hospital gown. She asked to come in and said, "I just heard your broadcast at the hospital. I feel awful inside—I need help." Audrey brought her a robe, and we both listened as she shared her fears. She heard God's Word, prayed with us, and found peace in her soul. Joy replaced the trembling fear that had haunted her face. "I have to hurry back to the hospital," she confessed. "I talked an orderly into lending me his car, and I don't want to get him in trouble. Thank you for helping me."

A Chicago businessman called me with dire fears: "My wife is in the hospital about to give birth. The doctors say neither she nor the baby can live. Will you pray, please?" I prayed that, if it pleased God, both would survive and good health would be restored. A few hours later the phone rang again. It was the same man. He was so excited he could hardly talk. "My wife and son are both doing fine, and we named him Michael. Thank you for your prayers."

We're deeply moved by many of the letters. Here's one example: "My father was pastor of a satanist church. He died. Then my husband became pastor and he died. I didn't want to live. I decided to take my life. With a powerful drug at my side, I turned on the radio to find some soothing music to die by. I found some beautiful music and sat down, ready to finish my course on earth. Then you started to speak. You said something like, 'Come to me you who are weary and heavy laden.' You said those words were from Jesus, and you promised if I came to Him, He would save me and give me rest and peace. That was what I wanted. I prayed. I called on Him. He saved me. I have had a life-changing experience. Thank you for helping me."

Every day God entrusts our work with the needs of people like these. And we've learned that it truly is possible to beyond measure. Responding to needs brings our energy up and keeps our efficiency high—whatever the hour of day or night. I think a Christian should call the alarm clock an opportunity clock.

Encouraging words and stories of results also come from station managers and newspaper editors who carry Michael's messages. The Guidos, who never charge the stations or papers for their material, find their reward and renewed energy in these responses.

The Guidos are fun loving and enjoy doing everything together. Theirs is a fruitful partnership. Their behavior defines unselfish and godly ambition. Each takes pleasure from the other's accomplishments, and both feel pride in the Lord and His continuing watchful care and protection.

ONCE DURING A midwestern revival I had a broadcast scheduled every morning from 5:30 to 5:50. We both got up and had our devotions before I left. One morning we both especially asked the Lord to alert us to dangers and opportunities. A few minutes after I drove away, there was a knock at the door. Audrey opened it, but she didn't unfasten the security chain, bless the Lord. A man stuck his foot in the opening and reached around to unhook the chain. Audrey, who had been pressing some clothes, used the iron on the intruder's hand and spiked his foot with her high heel. He screamed and ran. Nobody saw him after *that* pressing engagement! Just another evidence of the Lord going before.

Michael and Audrey share a strong sense of humor, even in danger, and they are living proof that God appoints the time for death. They are ever mindful of the accident that led them into this phase of their ministry. They know the odds indicated by the facts: Michael's three heart attacks and further surgeries; his mother's death of cancer at fifty-one; his father's death of a heart attack at sixty-one and his three younger sisters' deaths from the same cause; the deaths of Audrey's father from Parkinson's disease and of her younger sister from cancer. These are facts, but not deterrents. The Guidos' trust is not in facts but in the Lord of facts who knows the end from the beginning. The power of their partnership with each other and with the Lord has redeemed them from bondage to painful realities. Their wrinkles merely indicate where smiles have been. A seventy year old may have many years of productive life to look forward to, whereas a twenty year old may just have a few hours left because of accident or illness. Which is really older?

One new friend shared, "If you call their schedule exhausting, I would call it exuberant exhaustion. I never saw so much life in two people. After all, achievement is ageless. If you don't believe it, walk in Michael's or Audrey's shoes for one of those miracle miles."

THE BIBLE GIVES us an explicit secret for success—guaranteed by God: "This Book of the Law shall not depart from your mouth, but you shall meditate in it day and night, that you may observe to do according to all that is written in it. For then you will make your way prosperous, and then you will have good success" (Josh. 1:8).

Some may wonder if it is scriptural to strive for success in our walk with the Lord. Certainly! Our heavenly Father wants no failures. He approves of successful saints who realize that "only one life will soon be past, only what's done for Christ will last."

My mother's death showed me anew that "right now counts forever." She had been ill with cancer for some time when she went into a coma after brain surgery. My sisters helped to care for her, and Audrey stayed for several months to help. I traveled alone. We all prayed at all times for Ma's recovery.

When Audrey rejoined me on the road, we continued to pray for Ma's healing—until one night when I stopped my prayer in midsentence. I turned to Audrey and said, "Dear, here we are asking our Lord to heal Ma, but she isn't better. Do you know what just struck me? Ma used to say that when all of her children and her husband were saved and once Larry was in a Christian school, she'd be ready to go to heaven. All of that has come to pass. Is it possible our prayers are hindering her desire?"

We talked it out and decided to give it to the Lord. What great peace settled in our hearts! We went on to our service, but just as I stepped into the pulpit, I had a phone call from my brother-in-law back home. He said, "Ma has just gone to heaven." Her specialist had said that I must have released her for heaven.

We were deeply moved at her funeral. Ma was known for sowing her seeds of faith and kindness. For years she prayed, "Lord, give me every kid on this block," and the Lord did. Then she begged, "Lord, give me their parents," and He saved them. She had Bible classes for kids after school—six days a week—and the Lord saved many and called them into His service. The public school was dismissed early so the children could attend the funeral. One by one, their eyes filled with tears, they filed by her lifeless body saying, "Good-bye, Mrs. Guido. You led me to Jesus. I'll see you in heaven." Each child was a testimony to Ma's determined witness to everyone who crossed her path.

Audrey and I do our best to follow Ma's example and witness or give a tract to someone, but sometimes it's just not possible. We thought we might wear a pin shaped like a question mark so that when people asked about it we could say, "Where will you go when you die?" Audrey saved until she could have a question mark pin set with little diamonds for me. She gave it to me on our anniversary. And the Lord has used it to open the door to sharing and winning people to Him.

One day when our plane from San Diego arrived late in Atlanta, our connecting flight to Savannah was held a couple of minutes for us. As we boarded, a flight attendant noticed my pin and cheerfully asked about it. I smiled and asked, "Where will you go when you die?" Fear appeared on her face, and she ducked into the lavatory.

Later she returned and explained, "My father is a Baptist minister. I've been his prodigal daughter, and I've broken his heart. When you asked me that question, I had to admit to myself that if I died, I'd go to hell—in spite of my parents' prayers. I just called on Jesus to save me, and He has. As soon as we land, I'm going to call my father and tell him my good news."

The question of her eternal destiny was answered.

Michael Guido has been scattering *Seeds from the Sower* for most of his eventful life. He has no plans to slow down. He boldly shares that prayer is the cornerstone of his life, that Audrey is his unfailing joy. Together they use their energy and enthusiasm to refresh and restore those they meet at home and abroad. One such experience took place in the Panama Canal Zone. Michael's story is "vintage Guido":

I'LL NEVER FORGET the leper colony Audrey and I visited. A doctor who was changed by our program beamed to Panama asked to be our guide. While we were there, a woman leper kept her eyes on Audrey, watching her every move. When we stopped, the woman stopped. All during the morning, room to room, the lady followed, watching and listening while people shared how they were brought to faith and comfort through our ministry. We were curiously aware of her through all the joy in fellowship with the staff, the doctor, and the patients. It was so heartwarming to hear what the broadcasts meant. This made up for the many heartbreaks and heartaches of sowing the seed on distant, uncertain ground. Who would have thought it would penetrate this leprosarium? It made all the hard work worthwhile.

As we left, one of the lepers, hopelessly deformed and disfigured, said, "Good-bye! You led me to Jesus. I'll see you in heaven. But *there* we won't be lepers. We'll be whole."

I opened the car door, and the woman who had been following us threw herself at Audrey's feet. "Look at me closely, Mrs. Guido. I am a leper and I am pregnant. I do not want my baby to live and die in this death colony. I see Jesus in you. Please, please take the baby when it comes."

Our hearts broke for that mother even though we could not take the child. The experience constantly reminds us that our Lord chose us, not because we were attractive—we were not; not for what we could give to Him—but for what He could give us. He chose us and made us His very own. Audrey and I fell more deeply in love with our Lord on that unforgettable day.

Experiences like that move us on. They make us confident that Christians have no right to retire. Nothing would be worse than retiring from the work of the Lord who chose us. Our Father works unceasingly. Dare we work less?

And work they do, recognizing "the harvest is great and the laborers are few. . . ." They are a model Christian couple who are one in Christ, just as godly marriage was divinely designed. A verse from a wedding song by Jack Coleman describes them:

> Two shall be one, One with God the Father
> Two shall be one, Walking in His will.
> Two shall be free, Free to love each other
> Two shall be free, Walking in His will.
>   (Descant Music)

These two know the joy of walking with the One who has more answers than anyone has problems, more love than anyone needs. The God they know controls the present and future as He deals forever with the past. Approaching a half century of marriage, Michael and Audrey radiate an old Scottish proverb:

> When two fond hearts as one unite,
> The yoke is easy and the burden is light.

The future of the Guido Evangelistic Association is in God's hands. He is pleased with integrity and faithfulness and has promised to "shepherd them according to the integrity of His heart," to guide them "by the skillfulness of His hands" (Ps. 78:72, KJV).

Michael's niece, Evie Jayne Fontenot from Kinder, Louisiana, adds her warm and personal thoughts. When she was very young, she happily anticipated the times Aunt Audrey and Uncle Michael came to visit. The magic intrigued her. She has passed her uncle's meaningful songs and stories on to her children and grandchildren. She confides she is a blessed by-product of her aunt's and uncle's homespun teaching and the wide open arms extended to their family throughout her early years and into the present.

Recently her son, now in the ministry, read a statement written a century ago by D. L. Moody: "Who knows what would happen if a man was totally dedicated to the Lord Jesus Christ." Her son stopped and commented, "I wish I could get in touch with heaven and ask for Mr. Moody. I'd like to tell him about Uncle Michael. He just might be that man!"

A man accompanied by an ordained wife! Not with theological degrees, but impressive degrees and credentials. A wife who is still known as the "Magic Lady." One whose multiplied talents allowed her to step in to fill the pulpit for more than a year at the Presbyterian church in Metter when a pastor could not be found.

Audrey was the sharecropper's daughter who became the Sower's lady; Michael, the son of immigrants, catapulted to unsolicited fame simply by sowing good seeds. Together they are held by God's faithfulness and challenge us to cultivate faithfulness and become colaborers together with Him.

CHAPTER 15

CULTIVATE FAITHFULNESS

Trust in the LORD, and do good;
Dwell in the land and cultivate faithfulness.
Psalm 37:3-4, NASB

The Sower and his lady have no greater joy than to see other Christians bear fruit "in His season." The fine art of cultivating faithfulness has long been their trademark. They are convinced that as they personally *decrease*, the Lord will *increase* in their lives and fruitfulness. If the fruit of an apple tree is more apples and the fruit of a Georgia peach tree more peaches, then the fruit of a Christian must be—more Christians!

D. L. Moody often shared Horatio Bonar's description of knowing when a Christian was growing and bearing fruit: "In proportion to his growth in grace he would elevate his Master, talk less of what he was doing, and become smaller and smaller in his own esteem, until, like the morning star, he faded away before the rising sun." The Guidos believe that self is diminished and God "elevated" in direct proportion to a joyous sharing of God's grace.

Jonathan was willing to decrease that David might increase; John the Baptist displayed the same spirit of humility; Barnabas was willing to defer his talents and resources to the Apostle Paul.

Barnabas was called a "son of encouragement" (Acts

4:36), which was a simple Semitic idiom meaning "one who encourages."

Each of us while cultivating faith and faithfulness needs the reminder of the high calling of being "sons of encouragement"—encouraging others toward the Lord by life and spoken word.

Celebrating and sharing God's intense love for us should be natural, like expressing love to a dear one. The alternative of not sharing is not acceptable to God and resembles the story of a tribe of natives who were given a sundial. Far from civilization, they had never seen anything like it. Intent on preserving and honoring it, they built a roof over the dial to protect it from the weather *and* the reason for which it was made—the sun.

At times a Christian may resemble those villagers. Faith is put to one side and covered, keeping it from the "Son of Righteousness" and the purpose for which the believer exists. Clearly written in the Divine manufacturer's handbook, the Bible, is the challenge: "Say 'Thank you' to the Lord for being so good, for always being so loving and kind. Has the Lord redeemed you? Then speak out! Tell others He has saved you . . ." (Ps. 107:1–2, TLB).

Michael recalls how pleased he would be when his heavy schedule finally lightened enough so he could return home for a visit. On one such occasion, after he greeted the family, his little brother Larry crawled up on his lap and hugged him. "Larry," he asked, "did you like the gifts I sent you?"

"Yes," he answered. "I liked the boots. See, I'm wearing them. I liked the books. They are on the shelf, and I've read every one of them. I liked the clothes, too. I am wearing one of the shirts." Then he started to cry.

"Larry, what's wrong? Why are you crying?"

Hugging me tightly, he sobbed, "Brother, I liked everything, but I missed you. I wanted you. Now I got you, and that's all I want."

Michael remembers that day long ago as a challenge. "Now I got *you* and that is all I want!" It is easy for us to give God a little of our time, a little of our talents, and a little of our treasure. *He* desires everything. Pressing us to His cross-sized heart, He says to His children, "Most of all, I want you!"

Audrey recalls with joy her cousin Evelyn Warren. Through the years, Evelyn catered and provided countless special events, serving her cup of faithfulness beautifully and willingly.

WE CULTIVATE FAITHFULNESS by studying God's Word and praying. Charles Wesley said that "nothing is accomplished except by prayer." We pray promises instead of problems. Prayer changes things and people—including the one offering the prayer.

Memorize God's word so His word displaces yours, and remember—His never returns void. Meditate on Him. Let your faith glow and grow.

George Muller, the great founder of orphanages and faith advocate of years past wrote,

My faith is the same faith which is found in every believer. It has been increased little by little for the last twenty-six years. Many times when I could have gone insane from worry, I was at peace because my soul believed the truth of God's promises. God's word, together with the whole character of God, as He has revealed Himself, settles all questions. His unchangeable love and His infinite wisdom calmed me. I knew "God is able and willing to deliver me." It is written, "He who did not spare His own Son, but delivered Him up for us all, how shall He not with Him also freely give us all things?" (Rom. 8:32).

My work is not a trying life but a very happy one. It is impossible to describe the abundance of peace and heavenly joy that often flows into my

soul because of the answers I obtain from God
after waiting on Him for help and blessing. I pray
saints will be benefited by the dealings of God
with me.

Through the years George Muller's faith has been a
touchstone to Christendom. The Sower is his modern
counterpart. Both learned at the feet of Jesus that
faithfulness is cultivated in the Word! Prayer! Uninhibited
Faith! Joy! Consistency! Implicit Trust! Each felt blessed
in Jesus and needed no stimulus to do good works. "The
forgiveness of our sins, having been made forever the
children of God, having before us the Father's house as
our home—these blessings should constrain us to serve
God in love and gratitude all the days of our lives." These
phrases appear often in the writings of both men. Both
were willing to risk it all for Jesus.

The rewards? George Muller's fill many books.
Michael's and Audrey's grow.

At an airport in North Carolina a man came up, out of
breath from playing catch-up-with-Michael. He had heard
the Guido story on a Christian network and wanted to say
thank you: "Years ago when you held a citywide revival in
Illinois, a seven-year-old girl came up and commented on
Mrs. Guido's jewelry. Mrs. Guido asked her if she loved
Jesus and she said no. After a junior-sized conversation
with the minister and magic lady, she changed her mind
and became a Christian.

Some years later she met a hell-raising Catholic and
led him to the Lord. The Lord called him to preach, and
today that little girl is my beautiful wife. We've been
laboring for the Lord. You've taught us much through
the years. We've kept track of those who have been
converted in our meetings, and to date it is more than
sixty thousand. Thank you for being faithful. Thank
your wife for the magic. Thank you both for the love
that constrains your witness!"

WE ARE CHALLENGED to "go and do likewise!"

Some readers, recently encouraged or new in faith, may wonder just what a sower is supposed to be. The definition comes from Michael's heart:

A SOWER LIVES as close as possible to the Scripture in its description, attitude, and action of the sower. A sower is sold out to the Lord even as the first Sower was to His Father. Of course, we cannot be just like Him; we will never be perfect. But we can let His mind be in us and His will be done through us, and we can winsomely lead His recalcitrant children back into His family.

How can seed best be sown? Lovingly and prayerfully, casually and kindly, spreading the seeds in all walks of normal life.

One of Michael's mentors, D. L. Moody, expressed his method more than a century ago, of using incidents of everyday life, illustrations, and anecdotes. He told students at the Moody Bible Institute:

When I was preaching in Baltimore in 1879, an infidel reporter, who believed I was a humbug, came to the meetings with the express purpose of catching me in my remarks. He believed that my stories and anecdotes were all made up, and he intended to expose me in his paper.

One of the anecdotes I told was as follows:

A gentleman was walking down the streets of a city some time ago. It was near Christmastime, and many of the shop windows were filled with Christmas presents and toys. As this gentleman passed along, he saw three little girls standing before a shop window. Two of them were trying to describe to the third the things that were in the window. It aroused his attention, and he wondered what it could mean. He went back, and found that the middle one was blind—she had never been able to see—and her two sisters were endeavoring to tell her how the things looked. The gentleman stood beside them for some time and listened; he said it was most interesting to hear them trying to

describe the different articles to the blind child—
they found it a difficult task.

"That is just my position in trying to tell other
men about Christ," I said. "I may talk about
Him; and yet they see no beauty in Him that they
should desire Him. But if they will only come to
Him, He will open their eyes and reveal Himself
to them in all His loveliness and grace."

After the meeting this reporter came to me and
asked where I got that story. I said I had read it in
a Boston paper. He told me that it had happened
right there in the streets of Baltimore and that he
was the gentleman referred to! It made such an
impression on him that he accepted Christ and
became one of the first converts in that city.

Many and many a time I have found that when
the sermon—and even the text—has been forgot-
ten, some story has fastened itself in a hearer's
mind, and has borne fruit. Anecdotes are like windows to let light in upon a subject. They have a
useful ministry.

The Sower's messages in audio, video, and print are
sent forth in prayer. Prayer is an imperative. Michael
wakes up in prayer, walks in prayer through the day and
into the evenings, and covers every call and activity by
prayer.

For some years his schedule was so demanding that it
made it almost impossible to speak at all the Rotary clubs,
ribbon-cutting ceremonies, state capitols, or revivals.
During those years, God was impressing a young boy,
close to Statesboro, Georgia, with a love for flying. Short-
wing or fixed-wing, biplanes, World War II planes,
Cessnas, twin-engine jets, or just experimental, Ellis
Wood loved planes and made himself at home in airports.
Wood's introduction to the Sower had nothing to do with
flying:

WE NEEDED SOMEONE to blacktop a long drive and a big parking area and to advise us properly in draining the gardens we use for video taping. Friends recommended a reliable contractor, Ellis Wood. He came, measured the areas, presented a proposal, and then reminded me of a meeting I held in Macon at a church where he had been a member. It had been a real revival! Ellis shared his faith with me, then told me, "The Lord has given me a twin-engine Baron, and He has laid it on my heart to offer to fly you to any and all of your meetings without cost. May I?"

What kindness! I hardly knew what to say. I thanked him and said that I would be in touch. He did the work, donating tons of gravel and hundreds of feet of drain tile as a gift to the Lord. And he is flying me to my meetings.

The pilot and Sower accelerate down the runway, lift off, and soar over the pine trees, flying to another opportunity for the Lord. Ellis' competence and skill has taken them through all kinds of weather, slipping those surly bonds of earth, chasing clouds, and undertaking high flight for the most high God. Ellis loves his volunteer status and knows they travel on wings of prayer—from Audrey and his wife, Kathy.

After a meeting they rejoice in God's faithfulness as they touch down. To the pilot and passenger the reward has no personal or material gain, but the evidence of changed lives will lift them above the clouds on another day very soon to sow seeds in many cities and states. The flights are not just fun, but fulfilling. Not to log hours, but souls.

Souls? Yes, souls! That has been the Guido imperative since Michael's mother gave him never-to-be-forgotten advice. Whenever you meet a person or pass a person, try to see written across the forehead the Bible verse, 'For whom Christ died.' It will constrain you to think of others, to do for others, and to pray for others." Michael was just eighteen. The imprint of "for whom Christ died" has never worn off.

Through the years the Guidos have thought little of

self-preservation. Instead, they have mostly thought of
spiritual presentation. Cultivating faithfulness is a lifelong
process. The rewards await on the other side. Rewards
that include an eternal retirement plan on streets of gold,
surrounded by "fruit" from the seeds of life the Guidos
have spread. Rewards in the form of crowns promised to
those who have cultivated faithfulness and endured.

These five crowns are available and waiting for the
faithful. Every Christian is a contestant. But not all run
alike. They make a good start, but some slow down
because of weariness and others stray because of
worldliness. Every Christian may win, if he wants to.

Which of the crowns will be yours?

The Crown of Glory: "And when the Chief Shepherd
appears, you will receive the *crown of glory* that does not
fade away" (1 Pet. 5:4).

The Crown of Righteousness: "I have fought the good
fight, I have finished the race, I have kept the faith.
Finally, there is laid up for me the *crown of righteousness*,
which the Lord, the righteous Judge, will give to me on
that Day, and not to me only but also to all who have
loved His appearing" (2 Tim. 4:7,8).

The Crown of Life: "Blessed is the man who endures
temptation; for when he has been proved, he will receive
the *crown of life* which the Lord has promised to those
who love Him" (James 1:12).

The Crown of Rejoicing: "For what is our hope, or joy,
or *crown of rejoicing?* Is it not even you in the presence of
our Lord Jesus Christ at His coming?" (1 Thess. 2:19).

The Incorruptible Crown: "Do you not know that in a
race all the runners run, but only one gets the prize? Run
in such a way as to get the prize. Everyone who competes
in the games goes into strict training. They do it to get a
crown of laurel that will not last; but we do it to get *a
crown that will last forever* (1 Cor. 9:24,25, NIV).

A CROWN THAT lasts *forever!* By God's grace and with His help,
that is what we seek to secure. Oh, there are the times that our
load becomes heavy and the task hard. Then we remember that

the Lord will carry on His work. But He has invited *us* to help Him. What an honor! What an unspeakable privilege!

During those times when we need a lift, we sometimes visualize the picture of a football player, depicted in a lonely locker room. Discouraged and downcast, his helmet is at his feet, his face in his hands, and his broad shoulders stooped. The caption: "I quit."

In the upper right corner of that memorable scene is a picture of Jesus on the Cross. The caption: "I didn't!"

Audrey and I are more determined each day not to quit. We long to win those five crowns so that we may lay them at the feet of Jesus, who wore that crown of thorns for us.

May we invite you to join with us in renewed commitment to share the Lord. Someone's eternal future depends on *your* faithfulness.

BRINGING IN THE SHEAVES

Sowing in the morning, sowing seeds of kindness,
Sowing in the noontide and the dewy eve;
Waiting for the harvest, and the time of reaping,
We shall come rejoicing, bringing in the sheaves.

Sowing in the sunshine, sowing in the shadows,
Fearing neither clouds nor winter's chilling breeze;
By and by the harvest and the labor ended,
We shall come rejoicing, bringing in the sheaves.

Going forth with weeping, sowing for the Master,
Tho' the loss sustained our spirit often grieves;
When our weeping's over, He will bid us
    welcome,
We shall come rejoicing, bringing in the sheaves.

Bringing in the sheaves, bringing in the sheaves,
We shall come rejoicing, bringing in the sheaves.
Bringing in the sheaves, bringing in the sheaves,
We shall come rejoicing, bringing in the sheaves.*

*Words by Knowles Shaw. Music by George A. Minor. Broadman Press, Nashville, Tennessee. ©1940, Broadman Press.

Seeds
FROM THE
SOWER

Throughout this book readers are challenged to sow the seed of the good news of Jesus Christ. Jesus imparted His truth through *parables*—a method familiar to the prophets of old, a means by which people of all ages and backgrounds could understand truth.

Someone has said that a parable is "a story that is true to this house on earth, but with windows reaching to the sky." Jesus shared the parable of the sower to shed heaven's light on a familiar subject. Sowing seeds! Reaping harvest! His parables do not *protect* His secrets but *project* them, even as we, His followers and fellow-sowers, are challenged.

The soil on which the seed falls is not the concern of the Sower. His mandate is to *sow*. "My Father works unceasingly and so must I. . . . The field is the world." The harvest is God's concern. When His followers sow God's Word (which is the seed), a good witness (which comes by a faithful sower), the gospel seed will bear fruit.

Michael and Audrey Guido have given us twentieth-century illustrations of first-century truth. As has often been said within these pages, they are contemporary sowers, and God has blessed their seed—seed lavishly planted, tearfully watered, and often welcomed. They have had their share of superficial receivers of the seed and selfish hearers, but the good ground brings their greatest rejoicing. These seeds take on new life, the life of Christ, and then "go forth to multiply."

This *Seed Calendar* is a compilation of previously written *Seeds from the Sower*, copyrighted and made available by the Guido Evangelistic Association. These simple thoughts may be used in conversations, letters, holiday greetings, or inspiration throughout the years as a tool to plant and cultivate seeds in the hearts and lives of neighbors, friends, associates, and family.

When sowing, remember:

"The seed is the word . . ." (Luke 8:11).

"He who received seed on the good ground is he who hears the word and understands it, who indeed bears fruit and produces: some a hundredfold, some sixty, some thirty" (Matt. 13:23).

He who continually goes forth weeping,
Bearing seeds for sowing,
Shall doubtless come again with rejoicing,
Bringing his sheaves with him. (Ps. 126:6).

Sow liberally! Won't you? Scattering seed wherever an opportunity arises. On believers and nonbelievers, in all economic situations, to all races and people, being assured those seeds will germinate as God prepares the soil. For His Word does not return void.

TIME

Read Ephesians 5:16

What would you do, if your bank credited your account every morning with eighty-four thousand six hundred dollars, but every night canceled whatever you failed to use during the day?

You'd draw out every cent, wouldn't you?

You have such a bank. Every morning God credits your account with eighty-four thousand six hundred seconds. Every night He cancels whatever you failed to use.

You can't buy time and you can't save it. You only spend it. If you don't spend it well, you waste it.

Yesterday is a canceled check. Tomorrow is a promissory note. Today is all the cash you have. Spend it wisely.

Prayer

Keep us, Father, from wasting our time, talents, and treasures. Inspire us to live in love to Thee and all who are Thine. Constrain us to do only those things that honor Thee. Through Christ. Amen.

THE THREE TABLETS

Read Philippians 1:21-30, TLB

Someone has said there are three tablets to life: school tablet, aspirin tablet, and stone tablet.

The pessimist turns the tablets into stages: desiring, despairing, and dying.

The cynic describes them as learning, lamenting, and losing.

But the Christian says, "Living means opportunities for Christ, and dying—well, that's even better."

Because the Lord has given me life in all its fullness, life to me is a blessing, not a curse, and death is gain, not loss.

It's learning eagerly, laboring earnestly, and living abundantly.

What's life to you?

Prayer

Inspire us, heavenly Father, to make Thy will our will, not in sullen submission, but gladly and gratefully, for in doing Thy will and delighting in it is our joy. All these things we ask in Thy name. Amen.

DOUBLE THE DOSE

Read Romans 12:9–10, TLB

A wise physician said to a young doctor, "I've been practicing medicine for a long time. I've prescribed many things. But in the long run, I've learned that the best medicine is love."

"What if it doesn't work?" asked the friend.

"Double the dose," he said.

When others are irritable, touchy, or rude, love them. If that doesn't work, double the dose.

When others insult you, lie about you, or persecute you, love them. If that doesn't work, double the dose.

That's the difference between growth and decay, excellence and mediocrity, success and failure.

So "love each other," and always double the dose, won't you?

Prayer

Father, give us Thy love which never fails, Thy strength which never falters, and Thy faith which never fears. We long for a clean heart for our lives and a clear mind for our labors. Make us useable and use us. Through Christ. Amen.

SITTING UNDER THE MINISTRY

Read Psalm 1

Yesterday I met a man who said, "Something's wrong with me. I can't understand it, for I've been sitting under the ministry of a great pastor for fifteen years."

"That's your trouble," I said. "You've been sitting, when you should have been standing, or sowing, or serving."

I don't want to be sitting. I want to be serving. I want to be completely used up when the Lord calls me home to heaven. For the harder I work, the happier I am.

The Lord has given me work until my life shall end, and He'll give me life until my work is done.

That's true of you, too. So let your work be a challenge, not a chore; a blessing, not a bore.

Prayer

Heavenly Father, deliver us from laziness and listlessness. Inspire us to be winsome in our witnessing, diligent in our discipleship, and productive in preaching the gospel. Through Christ. Amen.

MARCH IN MARCH

Read Joshua 1:8

I look forward to the possibilities of this month and to the promises of our Lord.

His sun will rise each morning and His stars will shine each night. His mountains will stand and His rain will fall. His Scriptures will be expounded and His salvation will be experienced. No problem will be too big for His power and no person too small for His pity.

For our weariest day He'll be our stay; for our darkest night He'll be our light; and for our weakest hour He'll be our power.

For our grief, there'll be His grace; for our faults, there'll be His forgiveness; for our struggles, there'll be His strength; and for our wants, there'll be His wealth.

I'm expecting this month to be a great and glorious month. Aren't you?

Prayer
Into Thy hands, Father, we slip our hands. We yield our hearts in glad and grateful obedience to Thee. In Christ. Amen.

"HOPE THOU IN GOD"

Read Psalm 42:1–5

When Mother Teresa of India saw people dying on the streets, she dragged their bodies into her home, and she cared for them until they died.

But a strange thing happened. When the people with terminal diseases were cared for, they felt the love of Christ. Hope sprang up in their hearts, and they lived.

They're changing the name of their place from Home Of The Dying to Home Of The Living.

Faith can turn trials into triumphs. Love can change scars into stars. Hope can transform despair into delight.

The Bible says, "Hope thou in God."

Prayer
Deliver us, Father, from the doubts that dwarf us, the errors which enslave us, the fears that fetter us, and the worry that weakens us. Fill our hearts with hope and happiness. Through Christ, our Lord and Savior. Amen.

CUT OFF THE SUCKERS

Read 1 Peter 2:1–2, NIV

If you want a rosebush to grow, there are two things you must do. First, cut off the suckers; second, cultivate the bush.

If you, as a Christian, want to grow, you, too, must cut off the suckers. And what are they? The Bible answers, "Therefore, rid yourselves of all malice and all deceit, hypocrisy, envy and slander."

How do you cultivate the Christian life? The Bible urges, "Like new-born babies, crave pure spiritual milk, so that by it you may grow up in your salvation."

Life is an incline. If you don't go up, you go down. If you don't grow in grace, you'll go into disgrace. Wouldn't you rather grow in grace?

Prayer

Make us, Father, growing and glowing Christians. Keep us from engaging in any pleasure or practice that will make us unholy and unhealthy believers. Control, direct and guide us. In the name of Jesus. Amen.

"HE IS RISEN"

Read Luke 24:6

A friend carried two pigeons into his church. Each had a Bible verse tied to a leg.

The first, a fantail pigeon, was released. It strutted around and showed off its fine feathers, but didn't care about the message.

The second, a homing pigeon, was released. It winged its way out of the building and into the sky.

Thirty minutes later the phone rang. The owner announced over the public address system that his bird had arrived, and had delivered the message: "He is risen!"

You have a gospel message. Will you on this day just display it like the fantail pigeon, or will you deliver it like the homing pigeon? Which?

Prayer

Make us eager, Father, to join heart and hands with all who are preaching the good news of our loving, living Christ. Constrain us to carry on victoriously and faithfully. Through Christ. Amen.

MOTHER'S DAY

Read 2 Timothy 3:14-17

Reckless and rebellious, John left home and became a sailor. He wasted his life on pleasures and prostitutes, but his mother prayed faithfully for him.

One day, during a storm, death was about to devour him. He prayed, "Mother's God, Thou God of mercy, have mercy on me." John Newton was saved.

Through his ministry Thomas Scott was born again and became a great Bible commentator. Through Scott's writings, William Cooper was converted, and he wrote, "There Is A Fountain Filled With Blood."

This came about by the piety, purity, and prayers of a sainted mother. Well could John Newton say, "My mother's prayers have followed me."

Help answer your mother's prayers on this Mother's Day by turning your life over to the Lord!

Prayer
Father, we thank Thee for our mothers who gave us life and love, who cared for us willingly, who counseled us wisely, and who constrained us to come to Thee. Help us to honor them. In Christ. Amen.

I DIDN'T PLANT ANYTHING

Read Joshua 1:1-9

A neighbor asked a farmer, "Where are your crops?"

"Didn't plant any," he answered. "Last year I planted seeds and got weeds. I had a fight with insects and drought. Now I'm playing it safe."

What a tragedy! For while he was idle, his land wasn't. It was growing weeds.

Yesterday may have had its failures, and today may have its fears. But each day is a challenge.

What will you do? Will you play it safe and do nothing, and thus produce a wilderness? Or will you go forth with God, trusting and toiling?

He promises, "Fear not, for I am with you. I will help you."

That's good enough for me. How about you?

Prayer
Deliver us, heavenly Father, from our fears, our faults, and our failures. Grant that we may feel Thy presence and fulfill Thy plan for our lives. Increase our faith. In the name of Jesus. Amen.

FATHER KNOWS

Read 1 Corinthians 10:5–13, TLB

A man saw a little boy wait for his father to pile up boxes for him to carry. As he waited for more, he said, "Son, you can't manage any more."

"Sir," answered the boy, "my father knows how much I can carry."

God won't shield you from burdens, but He'll sustain you. They come, not to destroy you, but to develop you.

The Living Bible says, "You can trust God to keep the temptation from becoming so strong that you can't stand up against it, for He has promised this and will do what He says. He will show you how to escape temptation's power so that you can bear up patiently against it."

The grass is greener after the rain, and you'll be stronger after your trial. You'll see.

Prayer

Father, impart unto us those qualities of faith and fortitude which will enable us to meet and master the burdens and battles of life. Strengthen and sustain us. Through Christ. Amen.

THE BEST IN LIFE

Read Psalm 16

Socrates asked a young man, "Where can I find the best things in life?"

Plato thought of the places that had the best merchandise, the best entertainment, the best food and drinks, and was about to answer.

But the philosopher interrupted by asking, "What are the best things?" That changed Plato's life.

Many miss the best in life. They forfeit their future by putting self-indulgence above self-control, greatness above goodness, cash above Christ. These things thrill, but they don't fill.

Do you want the best in life? Try the Lord. Put Him first, and no good thing will He withhold from you.

Prayer

Father, we open widely the door of our hearts to receive Thy strength as we strive to put Thee first in our lives. Inspire us with a faith that is vital and victorious, vocal and visible. Through Christ. Amen.

HELPING GOD

Read Psalm 37:34, TLB

A mother asked her little girl, "Where have you been?"

"In the garden helping God," she replied.

"How?" she wondered.

"Opening rosebuds," she said.

Sure enough, she had; and the roses were ruined.

Some run ahead of God, only to their ruin. Others dictate to God, only to their destruction.

But the one who wins is the one who waits upon God; committing to Him, for counsel and control, all his deliberations and decisions.

The Living Bible says, "Don't be impatient for the Lord to act! Keep traveling along His pathway and in due season He will honor you with every blessing."

Prayer

Help us, Father, to leave everything with Thee, quietly and confidently. Keep us from running ahead of Thee and from lagging behind. Deliver us from straying. Grant us Thy counsel and control. In Christ. Amen.

"WHERE'S THE PICCOLO?"

Read Romans 6:12–23

Sir Michael Costa, the celebrated conductor, was holding a rehearsal. The mighty chorus sang and the huge orchestra played, but the sound of the piccolo wasn't heard. The player thought, "It's small, it won't be missed."

But the great conductor stopped the music and cried, "Where's the piccolo?" The sound of the one very small instrument was essential to the harmony.

God needs you. You may think your talent is not significant. But to Him it's significant. You may think your part is immaterial, but to Him you are important.

You're needed in God's plan. Play your part, won't you!

Prayer

Father, make us useable and use us as Thou wilt, send us where Thou wilt, and when Thou wilt. We place ourselves wholly and happily in Thy hands. Have Thy way with us. Through Christ, our Savior. Amen.

CAST YOUR BREAD

Read Ecclesiastes 11:1

While some children were swimming, one began to drown. The gardener heard the screams, jumped into the water, and saved the boy, Winston Churchill.

"We must reward you," said the Churchills. "Your son wants to be a doctor. We'll pay his way through college."

Years later, when Churchill was Prime Minister, he was stricken with pneumonia. The King ordered, "Bring the best physician!"

Sir Alexander Fleming, the developer of penicillin, was chosen. He was the son of the gardener who saved young Winston from drowning.

The Bible's true: "Cast your bread upon the waters, for after many days you will find it again."

Prayer

Father, give me the courage to dare to love others, to respond and run to help others. Make me a caring, daring, giving, working Christian. In the name of Christ, our Savior. Amen.

HIDDEN OPPORTUNITIES

Read John 1:40–43

Years ago an obscure inventor built a racing car called "999" and hired a cyclist named Barney Oldfield to drive it in a race. That car hit a mile a minute and launched their careers.

Years later the auto builder encountered the racer and said, "You made me, Barney, and I made you."

"True," he replied. "But you must admit, Henry Ford, I did a better job than you did."

People are waiting to be discovered.

Andrew found Peter and brought him to the Lord. He became one of the world's greatest preachers.

Why don't you find someone and bring him to the Lord?

Prayer

Loving Savior, inspire us to seek and to save the lost, to count it all joy to spend and be spent, to woo and win others to Thee, and to do those things which are well-pleasing to Thee. Through Christ. Amen.

PERFORMANCE!

Read 1 Corinthians 12

A sea captain and his chief engineer argued as to which of them was the more important to the ship. Failing to agree, they swapped places.

The Chief went to the bridge, and the Captain to the engine room. After a while the Captain shouted, "I can't make her go!"

"Of course you can't," the Chief answered, "she's aground!"

As with the ship, so with service. Your place may not be mine, but your place is just as important. It's not prominence, but performance that counts.

The Lord wants to do through you what He hasn't done through anyone else. Fill your place with loyalty and joy.

Prayer

Father, do with us as Thou wilt, and use us as Thou wilt. We long to please Thee and to be profitable to Thee today and every day of our lives. We pray in Christ's name. Amen.

END OF THE ROPE

Read Philippians 4:19

Weeping, a man cried, "I'm at the end of my rope."

"Good," I said. "Now you've come to the beginning of the Lord's."

Are you at the end of your rope for salvation? There's the Lord. He said, "Look to Me, and be saved."

What about the solution of problems? There's the Lord. The Bible says, "If any of you lacks wisdom, ask of God, who gives to all liberally."

At the end of your rope for strength? There's the Lord. St. Paul said, "I can do all things through Christ."

And supplies? There's the Lord. The Bible says, "My God shall supply all your needs."

Yes, when you come to the end of your rope, take the Lord's.

Prayer

Lord, Thou dost embrace Thy children with the arms of Thy mercy and might, guide us and guard us. Pour upon us the riches of Thy blessings and benefits, giving us Thy grace. In Christ. Amen.

"I WANT YOU"

Read Matthew 11:28

Alexander Graham Bell made his first telephone out of an old cigar box, two magnets, and two hundred feet of wire.

His first message was, "Mr. Watson, come here. I want you."

And that's the Lord's first message to you.

He wants you to come to Him not for what you can give Him, but for what He can give you.

He'll give you a life that can't die, a hope that can't be disappointed, a light that can't be darkened, a joy that can't be diminished, a home that can't be destroyed, and a rest that can't be disturbed.

Hear Him as He says to you, "Come unto Me, all ye that labor and are heavy laden, and I will give you rest."

Prayer

We come to Thee, Father, knowing You will not cast us out. Help us daily to come to You knowing those who come to You are always welcomed.

KEEP SWINGING

Read James 1:12, TLB

Babe Ruth hit seven hundred fourteen home runs in his big-league career. Just about everyone knows that record.

Not many know that he struck out one thousand three hundred thirty times. But he's remembered as the home-run king because he kept swinging.

The will to keep swinging is often the difference between failure and success.

So never stop swinging—in anything great or small, religious or secular—except to convictions of hope and godliness.

The Living Bible says, "Happy is the man who doesn't give in and do wrong when he is tempted for afterwards he will get as his reward the crown of life which God has promised those who love Him."

Prayer:

Heavenly Father, grant us patience and perseverance. Keep us from giving in to disobedience and defeat. Help us to do with all our might what our hands find to do. Through Christ. Amen.

"GIVE THANKS"

Read 1 Thessalonians 5:18

The royal court was grumbly, not grateful. It disturbed the king, and he decided to teach them a lesson. He invited them to a feast. While eating, in stumbled a beggar by prior arrangement. Finding a seat at the king's table, he gorged himself with the king's food and left without giving thanks.

Angrily, the guests asked to punish him. But the king said, "That beggar has done only once to an earthly king what each of you does three times a day to God."

A person without gratitude is a bird without song, a night without day, a tree without root, a bloom without fruit.

Heed the word of the Lord: "In everything give thanks."

Prayer
Thou art love, Father; make us loving. Thou art forgiving; make us forgiving also. Thou art truth; make us truthful and inspire us to be genuinely grateful for all Thy gifts. Through Christ. Amen.

THE VALUE OF TENSION

Read 2 Corinthians 12:1–10

Have you ever tried to play a violin when the strings were loose? Don't!

It was my first recital. I was about ten. I had tuned my violin. Everything was just right. But when my back was turned a rascal loosened the strings.

The teacher introduced me. The audience welcomed me. I started to play. Oh, it was awful. The strings were loose.

Tension is essential to lovely music. And it's essential to a meaningful life. Let it work for your good and God's glory.

Use it creatively and you'll have harmony, not discord.

Prayer
Enable us, heavenly Father, to turn tension into triumph. We beseech Thee to illumine our minds with a clearer vision of Thy word and Thy will, and help us to live gracious and godly lives. These things we ask in the name of our Lord and Savior, Jesus Christ. Amen.

A GIFT IS ON THE WAY

Read John 3:16

In the rush of Christmas shopping, a lady bought a box of fifty identical cards. She didn't bother to read them. She hastily signed her name and addressed all but one.

Several days later, after the cards had been mailed, she read the message of the unsent card. It said: "This card is just to say a gift is on the way."

God has sent sixty-six cards—the books of the Bible. They're just to say "a Gift is on the way." The Gift? His Son.

There are two sides to a gift—giving and receiving.

"God so loved the world that He gave." You will receive God's Gift, won't you?

Prayer
Father, we thank Thee for the gift of your Son, who was born in poverty that we might have the riches of Thy grace. Help us to cradle Thee in our hearts and to love Him with all our heart. In His name. Amen.

THE CROSS OF CHRIST

Read Galatians 2:20

There's a church in Europe that has a wooden door. On that door is a handle that's shaped in a circle. Inside of that circle is a cross cradled in a hand.

To open and close the door, you grab hold of the cross. When you do, the hand points at you. It seems to ask, "What does the cross mean to you?"

To me it means that Christ loved me and gave Himself for me. And

> Were the whole realm of nature mine,
> That were a present far too small;
> Love so amazing, so divine,
> Demands my soul, my life, my all.

Prayer
Thou didst give Thyself for us, heavenly Father; we now give ourselves for Thee. Make us what Thou wilt, send us where Thou wilt, use us as Thou wilt, and glorify Thy name through us. All these things we ask in Thy holy and precious name. Amen.